Paranormal
ESSEX

Paranormal
ESSEX

JASON DAY

The
History
Press

To Vic King, this one's for you mate

First published 2011

The History Press
The Mill, Brimscombe Port
Stroud, Gloucestershire, GL5 2QG
www.thehistorypress.co.uk

British Library Cataloguing in Publication Data.
A catalogue record for this book is available from the British Library.

ISBN 978 0 7524 5527 3

Typesetting and origination by The History Press
Printed in Great Britain
Manufacturing managed by Jellyfish Print Solutions Ltd

CONTENTS

About the Author

Writer and Broadcaster Jason Day was born and raised in Scunthorpe, where he lived for nearly thirty years until moving to Witham, Essex in 2001. Jason was the longest serving feature writer for *Paranormal* magazine (March 2006 to January 2008), the largest monthly paranormal publication of its kind in the UK at the time. He wrote more than twenty articles during that period. He has also been a regular contributor to paranormal publications such as *FATE* magazine in the USA (the longest running paranormal magazine in the world) and *Ghost Voices* magazine in the UK. He is also the author of the paranormal books *It's Only A Movie…Isn't it?* (Phantom Encounters, May 2010) and *Haunted Scunthorpe* (The History Press, October 2010). Additionally, Jason works with other figures within the written media industry, including some very prominent names in the paranormal community.

His interest in the paranormal was sparked by his love of film and passion for reading. Jason grew up on a staple diet of 'Hammer Horror' movies and the written works of Peter Underwood, Dr Hans Holzer and Harry Price. With the advent of television shows such as *Arthur C. Clarke's Mysterious World* and *Strange but True*, Jason was hooked. He decided to begin researching and investigating cases of the paranormal for himself and the fuse was lit.

Jason's experience working in the paranormal field has been varied, ranging from being a regular co-host on the *Friday Night Paranormal Show* on Pulse Talk Radio, to being the featured article writer for the paranormal reference website ghostdatabase.co.uk. Jason is also the Chief Consultant for the Famously

Author Jason Day at Kelvedon Hatch Secret Nuclear Bunker in Essex. (Photograph by Kelly Day)

Haunted Awards organization on MySpace. He has been a guest on numerous radio shows, appeared at several paranormal events and given lectures about the paranormal field and his work within it.

Jason currently hosts *The White Noise Paranormal Radio Show* on Blog Talk Radio and has interviewed leading figures in the paranormal community, such as James Randi, Dr Ciaran O'Keeffe, Derek Acorah, Lorraine Warren, Nick Pope, Stanton Friedman, Richard Wiseman, Ian Lawman, Jason Karl and Richard Felix. Now in its fourth series and well on its way to 100 episodes, the show can be found live online every Sunday night from 10 p.m. to midnight on the Blog Talk Radio website, at blogtalkradio.com/famously-haunted, or alternatively at the Official *White Noise Radio Show* website (www.whitenoiseparanormalradio.co.uk). Jason recently won two awards for the show at the International Paranormal Acknowledgment Awards, 2009. Jason was named Best International Paranormal Radio Show Host and *The White Noise Paranormal Radio Show* was voted Best International Paranormal Radio Program.

One of three founding members of a small not-for-profit organization based in Essex, SPIRIT (Society for Paranormal Investigation, Research, Information & Truth), established in March 2006, Jason's commitment to research and dedication to the quest of explaining the paranormal continues. In early 2010 Jason became Managing Director of Phantom Encounters Ltd, an events company offering a variety of paranormal experiences to the public, ranging from ghost hunts to UFO sky watches and monster hunts. You can find out more about Phantom Encounters events at www.phantomencounters.co.uk and more about Jason himself at his official website (www.jasonday.co.uk).

Jason Day inspects the writing facilities during his visit to Kelvedon Hatch. (Photograph by Kelly Day)

Foreword

I was delighted when I heard that Jason Day was about to publish his third book on the paranormal, entitled *Paranormal Essex*, and equally pleased when he asked me to add a word or two in the form of this foreword.

I first encountered Jason when he interviewed me for his weekly online talk show, *The White Noise Paranormal Radio Show*, which is now about to enter its fourth series and third year of broadcasting. I am a regular contributor to the show and have been impressed by Jason's no nonsense, matter-of-fact approach to the paranormal.

Not only does Jason cover the usual topics of ghosts, poltergeists and witches in this book, including Borley Rectory, Matthew Hopkins and Canewdon, he also covers the subjects of UFOs, mysterious creatures and other fascinating paranormal phenomena reported in Essex. I wish I had possessed a copy of this book when I was conducting research for my DVD *Ghosts of Essex*.

Jason has lived in Essex for the past ten years now and can surely be considered a local. I can think of no one better to write a book on Essex and its paranormal activities.

Richard Felix
Paranormal Historian, owner of Derby Gaol and formerly of
Living TV's *Most Haunted* (Series 2 - Series 8)

A Brief History of Essex

Essex is one of the home counties, located in the east of England, situated north-east of Greater London. Although the county is one of the most populated in the country, the sections of Essex located closest to London are parts of the metropolitan green belt, meaning that further development in those areas is prohibited.

The land which is now known as Essex was once ruled by the Celtic Tribe known as the Trinovantes, prior to the Roman Invasion. Both Essex and Suffolk were home to this tribe, who had grown wealthy through intensive trade with the Roman Empire. Trinovantian territory was the first to be annexed by the Roman Emperor Claudius when he began his invasion of Britain (the second Roman campaign) in AD 43. This included Camulodunum (Colchester) transferring from the Trinovantes to the Roman Empire as the capital of Roman Britain. Twelve years later, the capital was attacked and destroyed as the Trinovantes joined Boudica's Iceni tribe during her rebellion in AD 61.

A garrison of Roman soldiers. (Photograph by Matthias Kabel)

The coat of arms of Essex.

The name Essex originates from the early Middle Ages, which is the Anglo-Saxon period. It can be traced back to the old English word 'EastSeaxe', meaning East Saxons, the eastern kingdom of Saxons. It was during this era of history, more specifically AD 527, that the kingdom of East Seaxe was founded by Aescwine. The kingdom occupied the territory to the north of the River Thames and the east of the River Lee.

Following the Battle of Maldon in AD 991 and the subsequent Norman Conquest, the former Saxon kingdom became the basis for a county. In 1139, under the first Earl of Essex, Geoffrey De Mandeville, Essex became a county of England and gained administrative, legal and political power.

During the expansion of the railways in the Victorian era and the post-war development and growth of the county, Essex became a desirable place for workers in the city of London to live. With most of the towns and cities being commutable to the capital, Essex continues to expand and to all intents and purposes is like an extension of London itself.

With such a rich history spanning a long period of time, it is no wonder that Essex also has a paranormal history that is second to none. Having been home to what was once cited as the most haunted house in England and the former hunting ground of the notorious Witchfinder General, it comes as no surprise that Essex has often been referred to as the most paranormally active county in England.

So join me, if you will, as we take a tour of Essex and reveal a side of it you may not have encountered before. It's a place filled with witches, dragons, ghosts, werewolves and fairies – a county where poltergeists wreak havoc, doppelgangers are discovered, UFOs get spotted and people, on occasion, spontaneously burst into flames. You have been forewarned. You are about to enter paranormal Essex.

1

Monsters

The word 'monster' derives from the Latin *monstrum*, an aberrant occurrence, usually biological, that was taken as a sign that something was amiss within the natural order. The word connotes something wrong or evil; a monster is generally morally objectionable, physically or psychologically hideous, and a freak of nature. It is also used to describe something big or 'monstrous'.

Essex has a rich history of what can be termed as 'monster sightings'. Although the term can be subjective, many would agree that creatures such as dragons, huge sea serpents and bipedal fish could definitely be put in the Monster category. With monster sightings dating back to the twelfth century, the county has a wealth of legends and case files to delve into. Here is a look at some of the monsters that have, and possibly still do, frequent Essex.

The Horndon Worm

The Horndon Worm was a dragon said to have been imported into the country (presumably as a young serpent) in the Middle Ages by Barbary merchants. The term 'worm' refers to the species of dragon that this creature was said to be. Sometimes spelt 'wyrm' (from the Norse 'orm' and the Germanic 'vurm'), a worm is, in essence, a titanic snake. These limbless giants often grew from tiny innocuous looking serpents into terrifying dragons. However, unlike dragons, worms did not breathe fire, but spat venom or blew blasts of poisonous gas. A worm

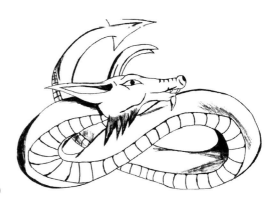

The Horndon Worm.
(Illustration by Jason Day)

would often poison whole areas, withering crops in its path. As well as having a deadly bite and breath, a worm could also crush its prey in monstrous coils, like an oversized python or anaconda. They also had the ability to rejoin severed sections of their bodies, making them exceedingly hard to kill.

Legend has it that the Horndon Worm escaped the merchants, who brought it into the country and set up its home in the surrounding forests of East Horndon in Essex. The creature grew to huge proportions and slipped in and out of the woodland, causing terror and havoc in the village. Eventually a knight, Sir James Tyrell, tracked the monster down to East Horndon Churchyard where the dragon was hiding among the tombs. Tyrell managed to dazzle the beast with the highly polished armour he was wearing, before quickly slaying it.

The Leigh-on-Sea Reptile

In February 1993, a long-necked reptile was witnessed by several people in Leigh-on-Sea. The creature, said to resemble a Plesiosaur, was seen swimming towards the sea in the northern part of the Thames Estuary.

The Basking Dragon

In May 1699, a dragon was reported to have basked for three days in a field near Henham. The description of the dragon fit that of a species which was known as a gwiber. The gwiber was a legless, winged serpent, which did not usually breathe fire, but had a highly venomous bite. This particular gwiber was described as being around 9ft long, as thick as a man's leg and with small wings. Its eyes were as large as that of a sheep and it had several rows of sharp teeth. Although the dragon was not appearing to cause any damage to property, livestock or residents in Henham, its demeanor was sufficiently alarming that a group of villagers, armed with farm implements and stones, chased it off.

A pamphlet regarding this incident, titled 'A True Relation of a Monsterous Serpent seen at Henham on the Mount in Saffron Walden' by Robert Winstantley of Saffron Walden, was published in 1699.

The Canvey Island Monster

In November 1954, the carcass of a creature was washed up on the shores of Canvey Island. Nothing unusual there you may think, but nothing could be further from the truth. For this was not thought to be the body of a dead animal, fish, bird or even an unfortunate human being. This was the Canvey Island Monster.

After a cursory inspection by zoologists, the specimen was described as being 76cm (2.4ft) long, with thick reddish-brown skin, gills and bulging eyes. The creature had all the initial qualities of a fish; however, it was also described as having hind legs and five-toed horseshoe-shaped feet with concave arches, which appeared to be suited for bipedal movement.

After the inspection, its remains were cremated, as it was said that it posed no danger to the public. No official explanation was given as to what this creature was.

Nine months later, in August 1955, a second carcass, this time more intact, was discovered. This specimen was described as being similar to the first, but much larger. It was 120cm (3.9ft) long, weighing approximately 11.3kg (25lb). It was sufficiently fresh enough for its eyes, nostrils and teeth to be studied. Again, no official explanation was given at the time as to what it was and no one knows what happened to the remains of the second carcass.

Twenty-four years went by and nobody was any wiser as to what the Canvey Island Monsters were, or where they came from. Then in 1999, fortean journalist Nicholas Warren carried out an investigation into the 1954-55 sightings.

Warren was unable to locate any official records to identify the unknown creature at the Plymouth Marine Biology Association Laboratory or the National Rivers Authority, but was able to find accounts from locals who believed it was an anglerfish. This determination was later seconded by Alwyne Wheeler, former ichthyologist for the Department of Zoology at the British Natural History Museum, who put forward that the creature was an anglerfish whose pronounced fins had been incorrectly described as being hind legs. Further research on the situation, however, has pointed to another new possibility – that the creature may have been an Ogcocephalidae or batfish (being that this species of Angler already possess leg-like fins towards their short tails). It is shown that batfish tend to also have reddish-coloured skin, bearing a close resemblance to the 'thick reddish-brown skin' of the creatures washed up in Canvey. Some researchers have come to the conclusion, therefore, that the Canvey Island Monster was merely an instance of misidentification of a rarely seen fish. Without any remains of the creature available or any concrete records from the time, all we can do is make up our own minds from the facts available to us. Was the Canvey Island Monster simply a fish? Was it a yet to be identified species? Or was it something far more unusual?

The Canvey Island Monster.
(Illustration by Jason Day)

The Dragon that Attacked St Osyth

A broadsheet produced in 1704 refers to a dragon of 'marvellous bigness' that was discovered in St Osyth during the reign on Henry II. Documents record that in 1170 the large dragon attacked a house in the village and that the air surrounding the creature was so hot that it set the whole area alight. Nothing more is known about the incident, the dragon, or indeed its fate.

The Westcliff Sea Monster

An interesting, if brief, account of a river monster was recorded in 1923 in Westcliff-on-Sea. In August of that year two crew members onboard a boat spotted something mysterious as they sailed into the mouth of the Thames. The captain of the vessel and a member of the crew observed a monstrous head perched on a snake-like neck rising two metres into the air from the river. The creature looked around for a short while and then simply vanished back into the water.

Death by a Dragon's Stare

The pamphlet 'A True Relation of a Monsterous Serpent seen at Henham on the Mount in Saffron Walden', by Robert Winstantley, published in 1699, relates the story of a basilisk dragon that held siege to Saffron Walden centuries before. The basilisk species of dragon was the smallest type of dragon, most of which were only 3ft long at their maximum length. What the basilisk lacked in size it made up for in deadliness. Its death-dealing powers came not from fiery-breath or tooth and claw, but from its withering glare. Any creature that caught the eyes of the basilisk would fall dead. There were said to be only two ways to kill a basilisk dragon and one was by using its reflection, as the basilisk's own gaze was as lethal to itself as to any other creature. Hence, its own reflection would kill it stone-dead! Equally, for some strange reason, the sound of a cock crowing at dawn would also kill the basilisk. The basilisk usually took the form of a small snake with a crest resembling a rooster's crown. In later stories, they looked like a horned rooster with the tail of a snake. In this form it was referred to as a cockatrice. The basilisk dragon seen in Saffron Waldon was described as:

> …not about a foot in length, of colour between black and yellow, having very red eyes, a sharp head and a white spot hereon like a crown. It goeth not winding like other serpents but upright on its breast. If a man touch it though with a long pole it kills him and if it sees a man far off it destroys him with its looks. Furthermore it breaketh stones, blasteth all plants with his breath, it burneth everything it goeth over; no herb can grow near the place of his abode.

The dragon was said to have killed so many people that the town was becoming severely depopulated. Finally, a wandering knight delivered the townspeople from the evil beast by covering his armour in crystal glass. On seeing its own reflection, the monster died.

A basilisk dragon.
(Illustration by Jason Day)

2

Mysterious Creatures

The term 'mysterious creature' could cover many types of beasts and beings that have been reported over history. As with most topics that are within the paranormal realm, pinning down a specific case to an exact genre is often very hard to do. For the purposes of this book this section includes creatures that I don't necessarily consider to be monsters.

Essex has many a story of mysterious creatures in its history. The county is full of stories of beasts, such as werewolves, fairies, black shucks, gnomes, ape creatures, elves and wild dogs. With sightings spanning the last 300 years, witnesses continue to report encounters with mysterious creatures in Essex to this very day. Here are some of the bizarre beasts of Essex.

Shaen's Shaggy Dog

Six miles north-east of Chelmsford, a creature known as 'Shaen's Shaggy Dog' was said to terrorise the village of Hatfield Peverel. On the Chelmsford side of the village stood a house called 'Crix', which was owned by the Shaen family from 1770 to 1858. The black dog is said to have roamed around the entrance gates to the property's driveway. There have been several reported instances of paranormal phenomena occurring around sightings of the creature and many have resulted in bizarre disappearances and even death.

A carter who encountered the hound is said to have come to a most unusual end. The large black dog blocked his side of the country lane and would not move. Wanting to chase the dog out of the way, the carter attempted to hit the dog, striking it with his riding crop. Upon doing so he was then immediately struck by a bolt of lightening. He was later found burnt to ashes next to his abandoned horse and wagon. Others, who have reported seeing the black dog vanishing, have subsequently returned to the spot and found scorched marks on the ground and a heavy smell of brimstone. Sightings of the hound became so frequent that the villagers accepted the creature's presence and following some of their untimely demises, they wisely decided that it was best to leave the creature to its own devices and so he continued padding away until a fateful day early in the 1900s. A new invention, the motor car, had found its way onto the quiet lanes of rural Essex. A motorist reported seeing the hound as he drove into the village street. He saw the creature's eyes as he approached it. Just as the motorist drew level, the dog let out a piteous wail and exploded into a mass of flames. It has never been seen since.

The Southend Werewolf

Mention the word 'werewolf' and automatically most people picture a cursed man that is doomed to transform into a monster when the moon is full. Howling at the night sky, he preys on unsuspecting victims with the savagery of the beast he has become. Most people would also associate such tales with small rural villages in Romania or perhaps France in the sixteenth and seventeenth centuries, when over 30,000 individuals were labelled as werewolves. It may perhaps come as a surprise to some then that there was a case of lycanthropy in Southend, Essex and that this case took place as recently as 1987.

On 22 July 1987, forty-four-year-old Bill Ramsey drove himself to Southend police station. He could not explain why, but he was in a severe state of agitation. Upon arrival he begged police officers to lock him up for his own safety and for the protection of the general public. Bill had never committed a crime or been in a fight in his life, so the police were naturally apprehensive about granting his wish. What ensued shortly afterwards would confirm Bill's fears.

While talking to police officers in the car park, Bill suddenly and inexplicably began growling like a crazed animal and lunged at them. The 5ft 7in carpenter grabbed Duty Sergeant Terry Fisher by the throat with one hand and threw the 6ft tall, 14-stone officer across the car park. Another policeman was scratched across the face as Bill arched his fingers like claws. Chief Superintendent Charles Harper recalled, 'The man was snarling, his lips were turned back and he held his hands rigid like claws. He seemed possessed of extraordinary strength and attacked the men with a ferocity that was frightening to all who observed him.'

It took six police officers to finally restrain Bill and eventually they forced him into a holding cell in the station. With Bill now in custody and partly subdued the police officers thought they had him safely locked up – they were wrong. Bill's frenzied attack began again as a huge crash caused officers to rush to his cell. Bill had smashed his head and right arm through the 1.5in-thick wooden slot in the cell door, normally used for passing through trays of food. The fire brigade were called in to cut him free and would only do so after Bill was sedated. A police surgeon gave him a dose of powerful sedative while he was still trapped in the door, but it had no effect. It took a dose of between one-and-a-half and three times that needed for a man of Bill's size to sufficiently calm him enough for the fireman to free him.

After restraining Bill once again the police officers were at a loss as to explain his behaviour and seemingly superhuman strength. PC Tony Belford, who was on duty at the time said, 'I've never seen anything like it before or since, to see a human being doing things like that. I felt quite sorry for the guy.'

The common perception of a werewolf. (Illustration by Jason Day)

Bill was ordered by local magistrates to be detained in Runwell Hospital for twenty-eight days and underwent tests for schizophrenia and epilepsy. Doctors were unable to explain his behaviour. Psychiatrists however believed Bill was suffering from lycanthropy, a condition where victims believe they are wolves.

Bill was unable to remember anything about the night's events. Everything he knew about the episode, he heard from eyewitness accounts. After the incident he worried it would happen again, and over the next two years he did suffer further episodes. Bill said, 'I was terrified of where I was going to wake up the next morning. The police station. The hospital. I didn't know what was happening. The major concern was am I going to kill someone.'

After learning of the incident, Bill was contacted by renowned American demonologists and paranormal investigators Ed and Lorraine Warren. They told him they thought he was possessed and arranged for him to travel to their home town of Connecticut, USA to be exorcised.

On 28 July 1989, Bill met with the Warrens and was exorcised by a bishop at Our Lady of the Rosary Chapel in the town of Monroe. The exorcism was attended by the Warrens, the bishop and two guards armed with stun guns in case Bill turned violent. As the bishop chanted in Latin Bill felt something stirring inside him. His hands tried to make a claw shape and he thought, 'something's going to happen here.' The last thing Bill remembered about the exorcism was the fear that he would hurt the bishop. He said, 'He was a frail old man. I could have killed him.'

Witnesses recalled that the guards fought to restrain Bill, who growled and struggled until the ceremony was over. Bill added, 'I came round and was pouring with sweat. I don't know what happened but it did the job. Whatever it was has never bothered me since.'

Since 1989, Bill has lived a quiet life with his wife Nina and their three children. Perhaps the curse of the werewolf was indeed broken by the exorcism.

Fairies, Elves and Gnomes

Whatever the name used to describe these little creatures, there have been numerous reports of sightings of fairies, elves and gnomes in Essex over the years. Most of these beings seem to be pleasant, although some have seemed to be mischievous and very occasionally there are those that appear to have evil intentions. There are legends such as those of Lavina, a female elf who can be heard singing on the sight of Gypsy Mead in Fyfield at dawn and Rollicking Bill, a fairy fellow who is said to skip over the marshes in Maldon at twilight. However, there are also reports that have a little more substance than just legend. These are the cases where there are actual eyewitness reports.

A case in point occurred in the 1960s on Victoria Road in Colchester. A resident of the street watched from their house as a group of fairies danced around an old tree trunk during daylight hours. They appeared to be happily playing and oblivious to the fact that the witness was observing them.

Depiction of a female elf.
(Illustration by T. Jacques)

Sightings of such creatures are not necessarily just a one off occurrence. Indeed, for a period of time there was a spate of regular sightings in the Broxted and Tilty areas. Locals blamed gnomes and other fairy folk for a multitude of tricks played on them and their property. There were many reported sightings, but these eventually died out and there have been no new reports in recent years.

The small creatures are not just playful or mischievous it would seem. From the following report it appears that they can also be rather industrious. In 1982 there was a report of a gnome sighting on the school field at Jaywick's Frobisher Primary School in Clacton-on-Sea. Two girls reported what they described as looking like 'garden gnomes', digging a hole in the school playing field. What exactly the creatures were digging the hole for we will never know, as the girls returned to their classes and never saw the creatures again.

As we have seen the playful, mischievous and industrious side of these creatures, I think we should take a look at the darker nature of some of these beings. A case that illustrates this well is the reports that came from Springfield Place near Chelmsford between 1864 and 1946. There were several witnesses that, on separate occasions, reported being harassed by an unknown force while at the building. Researchers, however, believe the assailant to be, 'an ugly, little, dwarf-like gnome', who is said to haunt the area, particularly the churchyard.

As all of these cases illustrate, there are several reported types of fairies, gnomes and elves and each, it would seem, with their own different temperaments. If you witness one of these creatures, perhaps the best advice would be to approach them with caution. It would seem that you just don't know what you should expect.

A typical depiction of a gnome. (Illustration by Jason Day)

The Spider Of Stock

Arthur Trumble was a renowned naturalist and botanist from Stock near Ingatestone in Essex. Trumble's lectures and talks were always well received and, following an expedition to Brazil, interest increased. Trumble returned to Essex from his trip to South America in 1777, bringing with him a vast collection of insects collected during his visit. Many of the specimens did not survive the journey home, but one that did was an enormous spider from the Amazon jungle. All went well until one day when Trumble reached inside his case to discover that the box he kept the spider in was open and the creature had escaped. The village of Stock was on alert and panic ensued. One unfortunate old lady was said to have died of a heart attack on the spot after seeing the escaped arachnid.

Sightings of the Spider of Stock continued to be reported for a further two centuries. Witnesses claimed the creature had been seen crawling up bedclothes, climbing up people's legs and descending from its web onto witnesses' heads. The reality is that a spider from such a warm climate would not have survived too long in the cold British winter and would definitely not have survived 200 years. So what were the local people experiencing? Was it the Spider of Stock or some other creature? The answer may lie in the testimony of Mrs Gloria Craven.

Mrs Craven lived in Hedingham, approximately twenty miles north of Stock. In 1974 she reported seeing a huge spider, 'the size of a dinner plate', crawling up her husband's jacket. She grabbed a nearby book and took a swing at the creature, striking her husband on the back of the neck in the process. The spider had disappeared.

Perhaps the answer as to the longevity in the life of the Spider of Stock story lies, in part, in this report. Maybe the spider is some sort of supernatural being, or even a ghostly apparition of the spider that Arthur Trumble brought back from Brazil over 230 years ago.

The Ape Creature of Devil's House

A very strange creature was sighted at an old farm known as Devil's House on Wallasea Island, among the marshes bordering the River Crouch in Essex. The incident was recounted by Eric Maple in his book *The Realm of the Ghosts* (1964), though he does not give a date or the name of the person involved.

The farm house had long been reputed to be haunted and finally, had a very disturbing effect on one of the staff at the premises. A labourer working in one of the barns heard his name called several times and every time he tried to investigate the source of the voice he could find no one around. As the calling continued he felt a sensation of coldness creep over him, eventually followed by an overwhelming urge to kill himself.

The man became entranced by the inhuman voice and picked up a length of rope. He then fastened one end of the rope around his neck and walked towards a ladder where he intended to fasten the other end to a beam. The labourer then heard the voice say, 'Do it, do it, do it.' He looked up saw a hideous ape-like creature crouching on one of the beams. The terrifying creature was thin and black and had bright yellow eyes. The man was so shocked by the creature that he awoke from his trance and he fled the barn, never to return.

A Satori, an ape-like creature from Japanese folklore that can read minds. A similar beast was encountered at Devil's House on Wallasea Island. (Illustration by Jason Day)

The Wild Dogs of Thundersley

In 2001 strange reports of wild dogs began surfacing from Wensley Road in Thundersley. Two large dog-like creatures were observed in the area. It was believed that they lived in nearby woodland and could be responsible for the recent spate of disappearing cats in the neighbourhood. Whether or not these creatures were wild dogs or some type of cryptid, has yet to be determined.

3

Ghosts and Hauntings

In folklore, fiction, philosophy, and popular culture, a ghost is the soul or spirit of a deceased person, taken to be capable of appearing in visible form or otherwise manifesting itself to the living. The English word 'ghost' comes from the Old English word *gást*. The synonym 'spook' is a Dutch loanword, akin to Low German *spôk* (of uncertain etymology). It entered the English language via the United States in the nineteenth century. Alternate words in modern usage include 'spectre' (from the Latin *spectrum*), the Scottish word 'wraith' (of obscure origin), 'phantom' (via French, ultimately from the Greek word *phantasma*) and 'apparition'.

Descriptions of the apparition of ghosts vary widely. The mode of manifestation can range from an invisible presence to translucent or wispy shapes, to realistic, life-like visions. Ghosts are generally described as solitary souls that haunt particular locations, objects, or people with which they were associated in life. However, stories of phantom armies, ghost trains, phantom ships, and even ghost animals, have also been recounted.

As with ghosts themselves, the places they are said to haunt are many and varied. From public houses to people's homes and from military bases to ancient castles and even nuclear bunkers, it would seem there is no location that is immune to a haunting. Essex is regarded as one of the most haunted places in England and, as such, it would be impossible to recount every ghostly encounter from the County in this book. In this section you will find a varied selection of reports detailing ghosts and haunted happenings in Essex, from both past and present.

The Phantoms of Moot Hall

It is believed that the Moot Hall in Maldon was constructed in the 1420s and was originally built for the D'Arcy family. The Hall eventually became a seat for power in the town and from 1810 housed a courtroom, which served as both a Magistrate's Court and a Court of Quarter Sessions. In the former role, it was still in use until 1950.

From 1863 until 1900 the ground floor was used as Maldon's police station and prison. Several cells were divided by partitions and iron grills. One such grill in the interior door still stands today and is witness to its former use. The position of the partitions can be seen in the walls by the existence of replaced brickwork. At the back of the Hall there is a small exercise yard that was used by the prisoners, which still displays examples of Victorian graffiti scratched into the brickwork of the walls.

The cellar at Moot Hall, Maldon. (Photograph by Jason Day)

The staircase to the courtroom at Moot Hall, Maldon. (Photograph by Jason Day)

The Hall also houses a council chamber and a clock tower on the roof. Although the courtroom, exercise yard, council chambers and many other features still remain, Moot Hall is no longer used for official purposes. The Hall is now a museum, an events venue and home to its very own ghosts.

Tour guides at the Hall describe hearing footsteps when there is nobody else in the building and experiencing the feeling of being watched. Guides also frequently report seeing shadowy figures gliding from room to room. The Hall regularly plays host to paranormal investigations and many attendees have reported similar experiences to the guides. There have also been incidents where doors on the upper levels have slammed shut when no one was near them and of people hearing banging on walls, disembodied voices and breathing. One of the most interesting incidents at the Hall was the sighting of a phantom figure seen walking across the exercise yard.

The identities of the spirits of Moot Hall are unknown. Perhaps they are former policemen or officials that worked at the old police station or courtroom, still performing their duties, or maybe they are disgruntled inmates, fated to serve eternity in the old cells.

The Disappearing Man

In July 1988 twenty-two-year-old French trucker Didier Chassagrande was driving his lorry along the A12 road in Kelvedon. Tragically, he hit a cyclist, who then went under his 38-ton DAF articulated lorry. Didier jumped out of his truck and found the elderly, grey haired man, bloody and unconscious on the road. He dragged him and his mangled cycle to the side of the road and then ran off to seek help.

Didier reported the incident to the police and returned with them to the scene of the accident ten minutes later. After searching the area, both the police and the horrified truck driver were astonished to learn that the old man and his bicycle had vanished. All that remained was the damage to the truck.

Spooks on Stage

The Civic Theatre in Chelmsford, like many others around the country, is said to be haunted. Visitors often ask members of staff about the friendly man who has helped them find their seat or directed them to the toilets. A chill comes over them when they are told that he is one of the buildings many ghosts. The considerate phantom is believed to be the spirit of a technician who was killed on nearby Duke Street.

Other paranormal activity reported in the theatre includes disembodied footsteps on the stage and an overwhelming feeling of unease on the balcony, the stairs leading to the wardrobe and the front of house office. Another apparition that frequents the building manifests itself in the form of a white butterfly. This spirit is traditionally seen every December during the show that is staged in the week over the Christmas period.

The Ghosts of Coggeshall

The village of Coggeshall is said to be one of the most haunted villages in Essex. Legends in the village suggest that a set of gallows were once located at the Tollgate crossroads, where public hangings were carried out. A secret coven used to meet at Marks Hall to carry out bizarre rituals and there are even rumours that the warrior Queen Boudica is buried (along with her chariot and treasure) somewhere in the area. Along with these legends there are perhaps hidden clues that the sleepy village of Coggeshall had a much more, very real, sinister past. Interestingly, St Peter's Road was formerly known as Dead Lane and East Street was once Gallows Street. Maybe then there is some factual substance to the claims that the village's sinister history is partly to blame for the wealth of paranormal activity in the area.

One of Coggeshall's most famous ghosts is that of Robin the Woodcutter. Robin was said to have carved an image entitled 'Angel of the Christmas Mysteries' in the sixteenth century. The carving was hidden during the Reformation, never to be found again. Robin's ghostly axe is still said to be heard chopping away in the distance by a brook in the village, which is now known as Robin's Brook. The phantom woodcutter has also been seen walking around the grounds of the Abbey, which is said to be haunted itself.

Coggeshall Abbey was founded as a Savigniac house in around 1140 by Queen Matilda, wife of King Stephen. She had inherited the manor of Coggeshall and endowed it to the new abbey. It proved an ideal ready-made site for the Cistercian order when it took over in 1147, having absorbed the impoverished Savigniac order and all its houses. Coggeshall Abbey was demolished in 1538 as the Dissolution of Monasteries swept across the country, although some of the abbey's structures did survive, mostly as ruins.

By 1581, Anne Paycocke and her husband Richard Benyan acquired the abbey ruins and built the east wing of the present Abbey House, around the remains of the abbey's infirmary. Of the abbey church and the buildings, all that survives now are foundations and buried remains, except for parts of the eastern wing, the guesthouse and the Abbot's lodgings, which still stand. According to eyewitness reports, a ghostly wrinkled monk silently walks these sites and ruins with a lit taper in his hands as he makes his way along old lanes, heading towards the Blackwater River. Phantom monks have also been sighted at Cradle House, a former haven for clergymen who held meetings in secret rooms within the building. These spirits have been seen dancing in the garden of the building.

There are several other spirits that haunt the village including an entity that resides at the White Hart Hotel. This ghost has been seen wandering around the older parts of the building (constructed in 1420), in particularly the guest's lounge. Little is known about this trapped soul and nobody knows the history behind who this may be or even which gender it is. The former Inn at 47 Church Street also encountered paranormal activity from 1966 onwards, when residents at the building reported odd smells, doors opening and closing of their own accord and a strange mist that crossed the base of the stairs. Another building that has experienced activity in the village is Guild House at Market End. A short, elderly man has reputedly materialised at the foot of a bed in the master bedroom and strange balls of light have been observed drifting around in the attic by independent witnesses from outside the building.

Some paranormal investigators believe that the cause of the incredible amount of activity in Coggeshall is the ley lines that cross in the village. Ley lines are powerful beams linked to the earth's magnetic pull and some people believe the energy caused when lines cross can provide the energy required for paranormal phenomena to occur.

Market End, the most haunted area of Coggeshall. (Photograph by Kelly Day)

The haunted White Hart Hotel in Coggeshall. (Photograph by Kelly Day)

The Ghost of Dick Turpin

Epping Forest has always been synonymous with footpads and highwaymen and none was more feared than Dick Turpin. Richard 'Dick' Turpin was born at the Blue Bell Inn (later the Rose and Crown) in Hempstead, Essex and was baptised on 21 September 1705. In around 1725 he married Elizabeth Millington. Following an apprenticeship, they moved north to Buckhurst Hill, Essex where Turpin opened a butcher's shop.

Turpin became involved with the Essex Gang. Initially he stole deer and in time began robbing people in their own homes. Following the break up of the gang he went on to become a notorious highwayman and murderer, before being captured and executed in York on Saturday, 7 April 1739.

Turpin's ghost has been reportedly witnessed on several occasions in both York and Essex. One of the most disturbing sightings of the spectre of Turpin is said to take place on the stretch of road near Loughton heading northwards through Epping Forest. The phantom is seen mounted on a black horse, galloping at breakneck speed with a skinny woman screaming and clutching at his waist, hanging down with her feet touching the ground.

Epping Forest, former home of Dick Turpin and the 'Essex Gang' and current home to many lost souls.

The ghostly woman seen with him is said to be a victim of the highwayman. Allegedly he tortured her until she revealed to him where she had hidden her valuables. Turpin then dragged her behind his horse until she was beaten to death.

A small body of water in Epping Forest known as the Suicide Pool, garnered its name from the number of deaths, both murders and suicides, occurring in its waters. While spending a night at the pool, a terrified Elliot O'Donnell watched a ghostly murder play out with the body finally being thrown into the pool. Was this an unfortunate victim of Dick Turpin or the victim of another phantom of Epping Forest?

Who is the Ghost of Feering All Saints?

All Saints' Church in Feering dates back to thirteenth century and was rebuilt in brick around AD 1500. The stone altar, which was built in 1961 by two parishioners, contains fragments from the ruins of Coggeshall Abbey, Walsingham Abbey and Colne Priory. The apparition of a man was regularly seen near a wall by a pulpit in the church during the 1890s. The mystery of who this man was may be just as intriguing as his ghostly appearances.

The story goes that the spirit is the ghost of John Hardman, a soldier killed in the Zulu war who was buried at Feering All Saints' Church. A search of the churchyard reveals no gravestone bearing John Hardman's name, although some of the stones have had their engraving erased by time and weather erosion. There is also no record of a John Hardman fighting in the Zulu wars in Africa.

There are records of a 678 John Harman however. He was a member of the 1st Battalion of the 24th (2nd Warwickshire) Regiment of Foot. Harman served in Africa during the Zulu wars and was killed at the Battle of Isandhlwana Hill on 22 January 1879. Perhaps there has been some mix up during the telling of the story over the years. If so the question still remains as to who the ghostly man seen to be holding a bloody stomach wound in the church is?

Is the ghost John Hardman and has his history been confused with somebody else's? Is the ghost John Harman and for some reason he is haunting the church in Feering? Could it be that the apparition is neither of these men and is another lost soul looking to rest in peace?

All Saints' Church, Feering. (Photograph by Kelly Day)

All Saints' Church graveyard, Feering. (Photograph by Kelly Day)

A depiction of the retreat, the morning after the Battle of Isandlwana during the Zulu War.

The Phantom Nurse

When new barracks were built for the Colchester army garrison in 1856 a twenty hut hospital complex was constructed. This was replaced with a fine looking red brick hospital in 1896. More building work was undertaken over many decades as the health care needs of soldiers changed and as medical advances were made. This included a pathology laboratory in 1934 and a reception annexe in 1951. Two operating theatres were added in 1963. In 1959, after the First World War, Second World War and the Korean War, the Colchester Military Hospital accepted civilian patients. The working capacity of the hospital had been reduced by this time and was down to about ninety beds spread over seven wards. One third were occupied by civilian patients and, by the early 1970s, more civilian patients were admitted to the army hospital.

By the time of its official closure in early 1978, Colchester Military Hospital was caring for 114 patients in eight wards and employed 150 army personal and 100 civilian staff. There is conjecture as to the date of the closure of Colchester Military Hospital – one date given is 17 December 1977, though some sources have stated 1978. There was a great deal of local support to keep the hospital open but it sadly closed and the building was demolished. Parts of the land are now a housing estate, while others are within Merville Barracks, home to 16 Air Assault Brigade and The Parachute Regiment.

During its time in service Colchester Military Hospital was said to be haunted. There were several sightings of a ghostly nurse in a Victorian nursing uniform walking down a corridor. She would suddenly vanish into thin air. During the Second World War, a patient reported a nurse in the same type of old fashioned nursing uniform changing his bandages. It was thought that this kindly soul was returning from the other side to visit and tend to her patients.

Ghost of the Airwaves

Following a move of premises during the 1990s from their former home at Layer Road, Hospital Radio Colchester encountered more than just a gremlin in the system at their new studios. HRC moved into its new home in March 1991, when new premises were offered at the refurbished Wilson Marriage Centre, formerly the old Wilson Marriage School in Barrack Street, which had been badly damaged by fire and had now been converted into a Community Centre.

The spirits began making their presence known by running across the loft of the building during broadcasts, but it was not long before they began taking a more active role, by joining presenters on-air. Staff recalled hearing a phantom choir singing and even a disembodied voice that seemed to call out listener's names.

Having moved on to new premises in 2010, it is not yet known whether the ghostly DJ has followed the HRC to its new studios or stayed behind at the Community Centre.

The Phantom of St Botolph's Tomb

St Botolph's Priory, located in Colchester, was the first English Augustinian priory church, founded at the end of the eleventh century from the Anglo-Saxon minster community of

The ruins of St Botolph's Priory,
Colchester. (Photograph by Kelly Day)

The haunted tombs at St Botolph's Priory,
Colchester. (Photograph by Kelly Day)

Colchester. At the Dissolution of the Monasteries, the priory buildings passed to secular owners, but the priory church passed into the care of the parish and served as a parish church. Only the ruined remains of the nave survive today, under the care of English Heritage.

In 1993 a young girl who was walking through the priory reported seeing a dark figure by a tomb. It smiled at her before vanishing into thin air. Subsequent sightings of a ghostly figure have been made in the area.

The Haunted Barracks

Colchester has a military history which dates back to Roman times. The first permanent military garrison in Colchester was established by Legio XX Valeria Victrix in AD 43 following the Claudian invasion of Britain. Today there are new and modern barracks outside the town which free up building land in the centre of Colchester and replace the old Victorian buildings. These new buildings are home to the 16 Air Assault Brigade, a major component of the UK's rapid deployment force. Colchester barracks is also the site of the last remaining military prison in the UK. Built in the nineteenth century, it has been modernised and renamed the Military Corrective Training Centre. Service personnel sentenced to detention there serve up to two years and are trained and rehabilitated, prior to being returned to active service or discharged into civilian life.

There have been two occurrences of paranormal activity of note that have been documented at the barracks. The first incident was reported in 1911 and involved three separate witnesses. On three occasions, three different soldiers were struck unconscious by an unseen force. These attacks all took part during the night and no perpetrator was ever found for the assaults. The activity ceased and it would be a further sixty-five years before the next ghostly episode occurred at the barracks.

In 1975 a corporal at Colchester barracks heard a door bang. The banging continued and the door was being struck so hard that it actually shook on its hinges. Moments later, the corporal flung the door open to see who was causing the disruption; there was nobody there. He closed the door and walked away and the door began banging and shaking again. Once more, he flung the door open and again there was no human cause for the disturbance. This happened several more times in quick succession before ceasing.

Considering the rich history of the site on which the barracks are built, it should come as no surprise that the buildings are haunted. With the military being based in Colchester since the Roman times, it should be more surprising that these are the only incidents of paranormal activity that have been reported by personnel so far. Are there more that remain unreported or indeed more to come?

The Warley Poltergeist

A curious report appeared in the Metro newspaper in August 2006 involving a family living in a council flat in the Warley area of Brentwood. The family began experiencing poltergeist phenomena such as unexplained knocking and the movement of objects. Things escalated and soon the family themselves were being affected, with the mother of the family claiming she had been scratched on the arm by the entity and the father being subjected to an electrical shock.

The final straw came when the couple's newborn baby was moved across the room by the invisible presence and the family fled the property.

The Haunted Fort

In ancient Briton a Roman garrison was situated in parkland in what is now know as East Tilbury, Essex. In Tudor times, a fort was built on the same site under the instruction of King Henry VIII. By the Victorian era the Royal Commission on the Defence of the United Kingdom had recommended that a coastal defence be rebuilt on the site and in 1874 Coalhouse fort was completed. The fort was positioned by the River Thames to form a 'triangle of fire' between Coalhouse Fort on the Essex bank of the river, Cliffe Fort and Shornmead Fort on the Kent bank, to defend the approaches to London against the threat of a French invasion. Coalhouse Fort continued to serve as a defensive gun battery for the capital through two World Wars and was eventually bought by Thurrock Council in 1962. Considered to be one of the finest examples of an armoured casemated fort in the UK, it eventually became run down and derelict. The Victorian gun battery was rescued by a group called The Coalhouse Fort Project; a team dedicated to raising money for its upkeep and restoration.

There are consistent reports of paranormal activity at the fort, so much so that the building has been extensively investigated by paranormal groups and ghost hunts are held there on a regular basis.

Visitors to Coalhouse Fort have, in the past, reported hearing screams and feelings of dizziness and nausea while investigating the 400 metres of claustrophobic tunnels on the site. In the very same tunnels people have seen spectral children and a terrifying figure cowering in a corner, moaning and shaking with fright.

Unsurprisingly, given the history of this location, many phantom soldiers have been witnessed here too. Sightings include military figures that have been seen running towards visitors and a ghostly Second World War poker game.

The fort is also home to a particularly malevolent spirit. The entity, described as a dark figure, has on more than one occasion thrown unsuspecting visitors to the ground.

Spirits of the Inn

There are many reports of phantoms and poltergeists haunting the numerous pubs and Inns of Essex. With several of these buildings being the focus of their community in the past and present, it is hardly surprising that they should be haunted. Coupled with this, considering the fact that many of these buildings and locations have hundreds of years of history predating that which they are used for now, it is almost a given that there will be at least one ghostly resident.

A case in point is O'Neill's in Colchester. The pub is said to be haunted by the ghost of an old man in a peak cap. The man is believed to be a former patron of the establishment from back in the days when it was the Wagon & Horses pub. The man has been seen on

Depiction of a poltergeist infestation.
(Illustration by Jason Day)

different occasions walking through walls and is said to be responsible for turning off taps in the cellar. Another ghostly old man is said to haunt The Black Horse pub in White Roding. This mischievous spirit was seen in the 1980s hobbling around the pub with a walking stick. The old man was also said to have been responsible for the strange sound of piano music in the pub, although there wasn't a piano in the building at the time.

The Beehive pub in Great Waltham has a rather different ghost. The spirit seen running down the corridor and disappearing into a bathroom wall, is not that of a human but that of a grey cat. The pub is also said to have a resident poltergeist, known as Old Ruffy. Old Ruffy is believed to have a habit of breaking glasses in the bar.

Poltergeists seem to be quite a common feature in the pubs of Essex and have been for a number of years according to reports. In 1956, two sisters were said to have left The Star Inn pub in Ingatestone after paying to spend the night in a room there. They hastily fled after the lights in their room turned themselves on and off and the door constantly opened and closed of its own accord.

The poltergeist phenomena continued at various establishments throughout the following fifty years, including an outbreak of unexplained noises at the Rose and Crown in Great Waltham during the 1980s. Builders reported being plagued by bizarre disturbances while carrying out conversion work at the pub, which is now known as The Great Waltham. Towards the end of the twentieth century, minor outbreaks of unexplained activity were being reported at the Ship Inn in Great Clacton. With the beginning of a new century another pub that experienced poltergeist activity in Essex was the Old Court House Inn at Great Bromley. During the early 2000s staff reported that several objects moved around the whole of the pub. More reports came in asserting that keys were going missing in the Greyhound pub in Wivenhoe. At the Duke of Edinburgh in Harwich, full bottles of spirits were being moved around and sometimes thrown on the floor and disembodied voices were heard emanating from an empty bar. In April 2009 The East London Paranormal research Society investigated the Mason Arms pub in Upminster, after a particularly unsettling spell of poltergeist activity. Staff claimed a butter knife was thrown from the kitchen, which was empty at the time. The investigators claimed that during their visit they made contact with the spirits of a sixteenth-century witch and a young boy.

It would seem that, despite the number of pubs and clubs being forced to close during the economic decline of the early twenty-first century, the ghosts of former residents and customers intend to stay.

The White Lady of Upminster

Upminster Golf Club House was originally a monastery over 800 years ago, but it is not the ghost of a monk that is said to haunt the building and the flat formerly used by the secretary of the club.

Several members of this exclusive golf club have, however, witnessed the figure of a young girl in a long white dress on the first floor hallway. The popular theory as to her identity is that the restless soul is a girl from Havering, who was kidnapped in the seventeenth century. She was held captive in the manor house (formerly the site of the monastery) and then murdered. It was believed that her body was then entombed in the room that now overlooks the golf club's car park.

The Faceless Monk

On 1 March 2003, three witnesses were terrified by an encounter with a phantom monk in Great Stanbridge. The onlookers reported seeing a figure wearing a cowl, moving slowly by the side of the country lane in their small village. As the apparition turned towards the group they noticed it was wearing a large wooden crucifix around its neck. The horrified witnesses fled in terror as they noticed the figure had no face beneath its hood, just a black gaping hole.

Depiction of a Cluniac monk, similar to the phantom encountered at Great Stanbridge. (Illustration by Jason Day)

The Old Woman of Hadleigh

During the 1800s an elderly lady ran the local village stores situated on the High Street in Hadleigh. Following her death in the 1900s, there have been numerous sightings of the apparition of a little old lady walking from the local graveyard in which she was buried to the shop she used to run. Witnesses have also reported seeing the lady in the shop through the window after hours.

The Ghost of Chelmsford Station

In 1995 Mick Cash was working for a plumbing and heating company in Boreham, Essex. During his time working for this company he was given a job at Chelmsford railway station. He had not worked at the station before and all he knew about the job was that a faulty hot water cylinder had to be replaced.

Chelmsford railway station, the scene of poltergeist activity in 1995.

On the first day of the job Mick was directed to a cafeteria on one of the station's platforms. One of the cafeteria's employees accompanied him down two floors, eventually reaching a corridor. The corridor turned back on itself and at the end of the passage there was a door to a storeroom directly ahead and a door to the right into the room where the faulty cylinder was situated. Upon inspecting the cylinder, Mick realised he had a couple of days work ahead of him.

The room wasn't very big – 12ft square perhaps. The cylinder that needed to be replaced was in the left hand corner by the door and the only other objects in the room were an old, solid table with thick round-turned legs and four chairs turned upside down, resting on the table top. Mick Recalls, 'It was certainly one of the quietest places I had worked in. Every time I put a tool down on the concrete floor the sound seemed exaggerated. I remember being very aware of my own breathing. It was quite unnerving at times.'

The first day's work was uneventful. However, as the job neared completion, things were about to change. Mick describes the incident:

Late during the second day whilst working on pipe work on the new cylinder there was a horrendous crashing sound from behind me. I turned around and saw the table behind me sitting up on one of its sides and the four chairs falling about on the floor. I looked out of the door to see if perhaps one of our other plumbers had done it for a bit of a laugh but there was no one there, I was on my own. I must admit that it did scare the hell out of me and I told my boss that I wouldn't go back down there unless someone else from the company came down with me. Another plumber was sent out to help me finish the job and there were no more incidents.

When the work had been completed Mick wondered how he was going to get the old cylinder out of the station as it was a large galvanised steel type. He had seen a pair of doors along the corridor where it bent back on itself, but hadn't taken much notice of them. When Mick and his colleague opened them, they were very surprised to find out that they were at street level. Mick thought he had been working below ground level, though he recalled having to go below into a room accessed by an old hand-made ladder. In this room there were no lights to turn the power on to the cylinder electrics. He found this room very uncomfortable, particularly after his earlier experience. Mick finished the job without any further incidents, but the unexplained phenomena he had witnessed has still stayed with him to this day. As Mick explains:

> At the beginning of the job, when I was being taken down by the woman from the cafeteria, she told me that she thought the area was haunted and that there had been many unexplained incidents in the storeroom next to where I was to be working, I thought she was just trying to unnerve me, turned out I was wrong. Many times since this incident I have wondered what had occupied the site before the station had been built. The end wall of the room I had worked in had the top of what looked like a reasonable size arch, as if the floor I was working on had been built above an older structure, I never did try to find out more about the site.

Perhaps it was a spirit from the past that Mick had encountered that day.

The Castle and the Quaker

Colchester was the first capital of Roman Britain and beneath the Castle are the remains of the most famous Roman buildings, the Temple of Claudius. The temple became a main target of the rebels led by Queen Boudica, who attacked the Roman town of Colchester in AD 60. The town's citizens barricaded themselves into the temple, but after two days they were all killed. After the revolt was suppressed the town and its magnificent temple were rebuilt. Around 1076, William I ordered a royal fortress to be built at Colchester. The great stone base of the ruined Roman temple was an obvious foundation for the castle. For most of its life the castle was used as a prison. One of the most infamous episodes in its history occurred in 1645, when Matthew Hopkins used the castle to imprison and interrogate suspected witches. Colchester Castle first opened to the public as a museum in 1860 and remains the town's flagship museum today.

Colchester Castle, former prison and now a very haunted museum. (Photograph by Kelly Day).

A replica of Queen Boudica's chariot at Colchester Castle Museum. (Photograph by Kelly Day)

A prison cell at Colchester Castle. (Photograph by Kelly Day)

Colchester Castle's dungeons lay claim to many ghostly sightings; these include witches, soldiers, children and former inmates. A number of these manifestations, however, are attributed to one particular spirit that is said to haunt the building.

James Parnell was born in Retford, Nottinghamshire, in 1636. During his formative years the country was in a state of great political and religious turmoil and numerous pamphlets, promoting different theological ideas, were circulating throughout the land. Dissenters from the established church risked persecution and imprisonment. Parnell studied the scriptures and became an ardent seeker of spiritual truth. Disillusioned with the traditional church, he left home to travel and seek out other religious sects, many of which met secretly to avoid persecution. During his quest he soon came to hear of George Fox, the founder of the Quaker movement. He was determined to meet Fox, who was then in jail in Carlisle. Legend has it that he walked 150 miles to visit Fox and came away fully committed to the Quaker cause.

Parnell began travelling south, spreading the word to all who would listen. His forthright approach to challenging the church led to several clashes with the authorities. In the summer of 1655 he reached north-east Essex, where he visited several towns, including Colchester, where he preached in St Nicholas' Church. Parnell reached Coggeshall and attended a fast that was being held to pray against the errors of the Quakers. After the priest had spoken Parnell spoke up for his faith, but he was interrupted. In the confusion that followed he was arrested as he left the church and charged with blasphemy and other offences. Parnell was taken to Colchester Castle and locked in the county jail there. During his trial at the Chelmsford Assizes the jury acquitted him of the charges. The Magistrate fined him £40, which he refused to pay, so he was returned to prison. The jailer, Nicholas Roberts, was known for his cruel, corrupt and vindictive ways. Conditions in Parnell's cell were terrible, and his treatment by Roberts was no better. Every time Parnell wished to eat he was forced to climb a rope by the merciless jailer and after some months Parnell's health began to fail, worsened by injuries from falling off the very same rope.

By the spring of 1656 he had become weak and for ten days he could take no food. Efforts of local Quakers to help him were barred and by the morning of 10 April he had died. He was buried in an unmarked grave in the castle grounds. A plaque commemorating his life has been placed in the castle, in the cell in which he died.

One visitor to the Castle was very underwhelmed by the supposed ghost of James Parnell that allegedly haunted the dungeons. The man agreed to a wager and stayed the night in Parnell's cell. The following morning the man emerged from his ordeal an incoherent, gibbering wreck and very reluctant indeed to talk about his overnight ordeal.

James Parnell's cell at Colchester Castle.
(Photograph by Kelly Day)

The Most Haunted House in England – The History of Borley

Borley is a tiny village situated in Essex in the south-east of England. Consisting of a handful of houses and a small church on a short stretch of road, there would seem to be no reason for anybody to show any interest in the place. However, Borley once held a title that many have since tried to lay claim to. The village was once the location of a rectory that became known as the most haunted house in England. The house saw five successive rectors, their wives, families and friends, all report witnessing paranormal phenomena in the building and was also investigated by one of the world's most infamous paranormal investigators.

Borley Rectory was a red brick, three storey building that was built in 1863 for the Revd H.D.E, Bull and his family. Almost immediately, upon its completion, there were reports of paranormal phenomena. From around 1885, there were sightings of a spectral nun within the grounds of the Rectory and in the following year a nurse who was employed by the Bull family left the house because of the 'ghostly footsteps' within the building.

Reverend Bull died in the Blue Room of the Rectory in 1892. His son Harry took over the pastoral duties of the village and continued to reside at the Rectory with his sisters. Around the year 1900 the four Bull sisters were out in the Rectory garden when they saw a ghostly nun walk towards the summer house, her head bowed as if in prayer. One of the sisters approached the nun, and as she did, the figure vanished.

When asked about the Bull sisters, paranormal researcher, investigator and author Peter Underwood recalled, 'They were much travelled, intelligent and educated people. They weren't fools and they certainly wouldn't allow themselves to make stories up to impress other people.'

The Bulls remained at the Rectory until the death of Harry Bull in 1927. Harry died in the Blue Room of the house, just as his father had done thirty-five years previously.

The Bulls were not the only family to have experienced the apparition during this period. Mr and Mrs Cooper lived in a cottage near the Rectory and this couple also reported seeing the spectral nun during this period of time.

The churchyard at Borley, haunted by the Borley Nun. (Photograph by Jason Day)

Above: Revd Henry Bull's Grave at Borley Churchyard. (Photograph by Jason Day)

Right: Molly Bull's Grave at Borley Churchyard. (Photograph by Jason Day)

Following Harry Bull's death, the rectory stood empty for a year, during which time a number of potential clergyman occupiers turned down the post. The Revd Eric Smith and his wife were the next people to occupy the house. Undeterred by the Rectory's haunted reputation, the self-professed sceptics moved in. Shortly after they took up residence the Smiths began hearing strange footsteps, voices and bells ringing of their own accord. As the phenomena escalated into the physical movement of objects, Mrs Smith began to doubt her own sanity. It was at this point that the Smiths contacted a national newspaper, the *Daily Mirror*, for help. The editor of the *Daily Mirror* decided to send along reporter V.C. Wall to write a feature on the strange goings on at Borley Rectory, and also invited renowned ghost hunter Harry Price to accompany him.

Harry was a former engineer who married a rich wife, enabling him to spend his time, and her money, investigating the paranormal. Price accepted the *Daily Mirror's* invitation and on 12 June 1929 he and his secretary Lucie Kaye arrived at Borley Rectory.

The Smiths relayed their experiences to Price and he also interviewed staff and others about their experiences at the house. He compiled a list that charted fifty years of strange happenings, including temperature changes, singing, strange voices, footsteps, smashed crockery, strange smells, the sound of coaches and galloping horses outside the building, banging doors and unexplained bell ringing. Price asked the Smiths if he could stay at the rectory for a few days and his investigation began.

If Harry Price had held any doubts about the building on his first evening there, he was about to experience the phenomena himself first hand. On that night he witnessed a number of paranormal phenomena, including having a narrow escape from a flying candlestick that fell towards him and *Daily Mirror* reporter V.C. Wall from the staircase above. Price himself noted, 'Although I have investigated many haunted houses before and since, never have such phenomena so impressed me as they did on this historic day. Sixteen hours of thrills.'

During his investigation Price also held a séance in the Blue Room. Allegedly he and others present heard faint tapping noises that responded to the questions asked during the session.

The spirit that was contacted during the séance identified itself as Harry Bull and told those present that he wished to attract attention to himself.

Harry Price left and his findings were released in the *Daily Mirror*. The Smiths themselves left the rectory not too long after Price's investigation after what had been, for them, an eventful three year occupancy.

In October 1930 Revd Lionel Foyster and his wife Marianne took over the rectory. Life in the quiet village of Borley was hardly Marianne's style – she was young enough to have been her husband's daughter and having moved from London to Borley, she missed the hustle and

Harry Price, ghost hunter and investigator of Borley Rectory.

The gateway to Borley Rectory grounds. (Photograph by Jason Day)

excitement. However, some would suggest the paranormal events at the rectory were very much to her liking. Alan Wesencraft, who knew Harry Price, theorised that, 'The poor girl really craved something a little more exciting and she found excitement, I think, by playing up the idea of the haunts.'

Shortly after moving in the Foysters claimed to be experiencing poltergeist phenomena. These events included glasses being smashed, mysterious writing appearing on walls and stones being thrown. Marianne Foyster seemed to be the focus for the poltergeist and as the activity reached its most violent peak in June 1931, she even claimed to have been thrown from her bed by an invisible force.

There were suspicions that Revd Foyster was being taken in by his wife and some thought this could be justified. In his diary he claimed his wife found pebbles under her pillow and objects, ranging from sticks to coal, were thrown at him. All of which could have been events manufactured by Marianne herself, or could have been a collusion between both parties.

However, there was also testimony from independent witnesses at this time. A local headmaster and magistrate, Guy L'Estrange, wrote of his experience taking afternoon tea with the Foysters at the rectory. As the three of them sat by the fire they heard a crash from the hallway outside. L'Estrange wrote, 'Jumping up I went to the door and found the floor outside littered with broken crockery.'

Still sceptical of the event, L'Estrange followed the Foysters back into the room where they closed the door and sat down by the fire again. No sooner had they done so when there was another violent disturbance. L'Estrange explained, 'An appalling series of crashes took us back to the doorway. Bottles were being thrown about in all directions in the hallway and nobody could be seen throwing them.'

The volume of phenomena the Foysters were claiming to experience led to Harry Price returning to the rectory in October 1931. As with his first visit, during the Revd Smith's occupancy, Price recorded a vast array of paranormal activity, including objects moving, doors opening and closing, locking and unlocking, noises, voices, strange smells and several other phenomena. Between October 1929 and January 1932 Price claimed that over 2,000 paranormal incidents had taken place at the rectory.

Alan Wesencraft suspected there may have been a rational conclusion to some of the claims during this time. He said, 'I think Harry Price's enthusiasm did lead him into making exaggerated claims. He had a fertile imagination and this would take charge I suppose.'

The most interesting part of the haunting during the Foysters time at the Rectory was the writing that appeared on the walls and the pieces of paper that Marianne claimed had come from nowhere. Years later, paranormal investigator Peter Underwood submitted these pieces of evidence to a professional graphologist whose findings were that Marianne Foyster had produced all of the writing herself. There was one exception to this – the word 'Edwin'. In the experts opinion this word was not written by Marianne.

Marianne had herself admitted to Harry Price that she hated Borley Rectory and wanted to leave. This revelation, coupled with the fact that most of the poltergeist activity occurred around Marianne, led Price to believe that she was perhaps producing much of the so-called phenomena herself. Price even went as far as to tell Lionel Foyster this himself.

After five years, the Foysters left the rectory and from October 1935 until May 1937 the house was unoccupied. With a lack of interest from the clergy it was Harry Price, who at this point took a year long lease of the property in order to investigate it himself more thoroughly. He placed an advertisement in *The Times*, inviting people of 'leisure and intelligence' who were also 'critical and unbiased', to assist him in his investigation. Price formed a team of investigators and drew up a plan for carrying out vigils and reporting phenomena. The team used remote-controlled movie cameras, tape measures and drew chalk lines around every moveable object, as well as various other procedures and experiments. Charles Wintour, who was later to become a distinguished newspaper editor, was one of the investigators who assisted Harry Price during the investigation. Wintour recalled:

> I went to Borley Rectory with an entirely open mind, I was just curious as to what was happening there. I was convinced that Harry Price was egging it on a bit There was something occurring but he was making it more so. In order to make sure that nobody was interfering with the house we would place cotton thread across the doors and across the passages so that nobody could sneak up.

On one occasion when Charles Wintour and his fellow investigator had returned to one such room, they found the seals in tact. Upon inspection of the room they were astonished to find marks on the walls inside, which included scratches and indecipherable messages.

Wintour recalled, 'On one occasion I thought one of the pencil marks was actually moving as I saw it. It seemed mad but I think that's what I saw.'

Other paranormal phenomena that allegedly occurred during the investigation included the movement of objects from their documented locations and the sounds of footsteps. In comparison to the previous reports made during the Smith's and the Foyster's time at Borley, Harry Price's year-long investigation seemed tame. There were no instances of poltergeist activity to report of.

The most interesting and controversial evidence to come from this investigation was the information alleged to have been obtained by Harry Price's lead investigator's daughter. S.H. Glanville's daughter claimed to have discovered the identity of the ghostly nun through the means of using a planchette to conduct automatic writing. Glanville's daughter said the nun's name was Marie Lairre. Marie came to Borley from a convent in Le Harrve, France. Tragically, Marie was murdered by a member of the Waldergrave family who were local landowners. Her body was then buried in the vicinity of the rectory. Marie was haunting the rectory as she wanted a Mass and a proper burial, as she had not received this following her murder on 17 May 1667.

The investigation concluded in May 1938 and Harry Price deduced that there were at least 100 witnesses to various phenomena. He said that he believed there was a poltergeist present at the rectory, but this did not explain the apparitions of the nun. Price concluded that no single theory could explain all the paranormal activity reported at Borley. Harry Price reaped the rewards of his research. His findings were published in a best-selling book and Borley Rectory became famously known as the most haunted house in England.

On 27 February 1939, Borley Rectory burned down. Captain Gregson, who owned the building at the time, was sorting books in the hall when he knocked a stack of books over which in turn disturbed a paraffin lamp, thus causing the fire. Gregson had also reported paranormal activity during his occupancy of the rectory. Interestingly the Blue Room, arguably the most haunted room in the building, was the first part of the house to burn.

Harry Price's book, *The Most Haunted House in England*, would prove to be the trigger for the next chapter in the history of Borley. Following his reading of the book Cannon Phythian Adams came up with a theory. Adams believed that his interpretation of one of the writings on the wall in the rectory suggested the remains of the murdered nun lay under the ruins of the rectory.

In 1943 Harry price returned to Borley and began digging up one the floor in one of the cellars. Incredibly parts of the skull of a young man or woman were found. Although the identity of the remains were impossible to establish, masses were said for the repose of Marie Lairre and pieces of skull were buried in a nearby churchyard in Liston two years later.

More intrigue was to follow, as the labourer who assisted with the burial had told the villagers at Borley that he was convinced they had only found pig remains in the cellar. This theory was also relayed by others, who claimed Harry Price had turned these into the story of being the nun's bones in order to create publicity for his second book on Borley, which was in the making. A second book did come. In 1946 Harry Price had his work *The End of Borley Rectory*, published. Price never claimed the bones he discovered were those of the nun, nor did he even accept any of the theories regarding her existence. He did however go on to say in the book, 'The Borley phenomena occurred in the way they were said to occur. They were of paranormal origin.

They have been scientifically proved... fraud, mal-observation, exaggeration, natural causes and trickery, conscious, unconscious or subconscious could not have accounted for them.'

Harry Price died two years later in 1948. Price went to the grave believing he had presented one of the most conclusive cases of proof of the existence of the paranormal. What had remained of Borley Rectory, that being ruins (after the fire), were demolished in 1944. With the rectory gone and the nun laid to rest, the haunting was thought to be over.

Following his death critics were also tearing apart Harry Price's work, claiming he had over exaggerated his findings, therefore discrediting the notion there was anything paranormal going on in Borley in the first place. Yet there were still those that were respected in the field that disagreed. Legendary paranormal investigator and researcher Peter Underwood said, 'There were things going on at Borley long before Marianne (Foyster) went there, and things going on long before Harry Price went there. There were things happening at Borley long after Marianne (Foyster) had left and long after Harry Price was dead.'

The reports did continue. In 1954 newspaper accounts reported sightings of apparitions around the site where the old rectory once stood. Residents still continued to verify paranormal phenomena occurring in the village too. Mrs Henning, the widow of the Rector of Lyston-cum-Borley, said:

> I lived near the rectory and the church from March to December 1936 and in the adjacent village for nineteen years. I maintain there is a great deal of evidence that the rectory was haunted before Mr Price ever visited it and certainly after Mrs Foyster had left.

The ruins of Borley Rectory following the fire and shortly before they were demolished.

Another former resident, Geoff Brown, also has no doubt as to the authenticity of the Borley claims. Brown stated, 'I've been involved with Borley for over forty years, including twenty-seven as editor of the local newspaper and in every one of those forty years something has been reported as happening at Borley.'

Brown also shed some light as to why the haunted occurrences continue, even after the ghost of the Borley Nun has supposedly been laid to rest. Brown suggests that the man who helped Harry Price bury Marie Lairre may have helped keep her spirit alive afterwards. Brown said:

> He was the one who, more than anyone else, moved the ghost from one side of the road to the other. He was the man who said, you know, strange things are happening in my church, I've seen things in my church and because he was a rector people believed him.

It is in the medieval church, across the road from the former site of Borley Rectory, that the paranormal activity was being reported. Witnesses claimed to experience unexplained happenings both in the grounds and inside the church itself.

During the 1990s, paranormal investigator Ron Russell was following in the footsteps of Harry Price and carrying out an investigation of Borley Church. One night Ron and a small team set up sound recording equipment inside the building. Ron said, 'To our surprise we received strange unaccountable noises on the tapes. I've no doubt that these sounds are paranormal.'

Another account of paranormal activity in the village was also reported in the 1990s, this time from Borley residents Pamela and Lucille Bullock. Pamela reported, 'I just heard what sounded like an organ playing from inside the church, but as we went into the church it suddenly stopped. To our amazement there wasn't a soul in the church. The organ console was closed and padlocked.'

Fellow witness Lucille Bullock added, 'Once we were inside the church we carried on looking around when I was aware of the sound of pebbles falling down on the ground. I looked but I couldn't see any pebbles.'

As with many of the stories surrounding Borley there is an explanation, albeit an incomplete one. Geoff Brown, former editor of the local newspaper explained:

> Some local boys confessed that they'd been hiding in the church. One of them pumped the organ up and the other one played a few bars. Then they dived behind the pews. Since then, in recent times, the church has been locked and still people are hearing the organ. What do you make of that?

As we entered a new millennium Borley's reputation was not forgotten and reports of paranormal phenomena in the village continue to flood in.

In 2002 two workmen using electric drills needed to bring power to their equipment from Borley Church, via a heavy duty extension cable, into the churchyard where they were working. For no reason that they were aware of, when they went to use their drills there was no power. When they went back to the power points in the church that the extension lead was plugged into, they found the plugs were disconnected. After placing the plugs back into the sockets and

going out to use the drills, they once again found them not to be working. A return visit to the power points in the church revealed the plugs had been disconnected again. This sequence of events was repeated several times, with no apparent cause for the ongoing disconnections.

A year later in 2003 the occupants of one of the properties built on the land that was formerly the site of Borley Rectory's garden reported poltergeist activity in their kitchen.

Even as recently as 2005 another resident of the village, whose house is located close to where the rectory once stood, claimed to hear the sound of breathing following her as she walked in her garden at dusk.

So the question remains, if Harry Price has laid the ghostly nun of Borley to rest and the rectory is no longer there, who or what still haunts the village of Borley, the church yard and the church itself and why?

One theory is that it is indeed a nun that haunts the village, but not that of Marie Lairre who was allegedly murdered in 1667. Some believe that the Borley Nun hails from an even earlier age. This particular story goes that the nun hailed from the thirteenth century and that she came from a convent close to Borley. The nun intended to elope with a monk from the village. On the fateful night of their planned escape the couple had enlisted the help of another monk and a coach and horses. They were captured and the monk was hanged. The nun met an even grimmer demise and was sealed alive within one of the monastery walls. Another version of the story claims that on the night of their escape the couple argued and the monk strangled the nun within the monastery grounds.

Whoever the nun may be and wherever she may have come from, legend still has it that on the evening of 28 July every year the nun takes what has come to be known as 'the nun's walk'. She begins her journey from the grounds of Borley Church and walks down the road, pausing for a rest against gate-posts, before continuing along her path, eventually disappearing into thin air.

There is no doubt that the tiny village of Borley is steeped in a long history of the paranormal. There can be no doubt either that the haunting of Borley Rectory during the 1920s and 1930s is one of the most famous cases of alleged paranormal activity in Britain and indeed the world. Whether there will ever be another Borley remains to be seen. Many buildings claim to be the most haunted house in England, but the one that turned a tiny village in Essex into the haunted Mecca of the country may just have actually warranted the title.

One thing is for sure, the haunted history of Borley will no doubt continue long into the future.

The Phantom Airmen of Hadstock

On a November afternoon in 1943, Captain Robert Scholz of the 8th USAAF was returning to Little Walden airfield in his Mustang fighter plane. Schultz had developed engine trouble over the Channel, but had managed to reach the base. The emergency services waited anxiously as he circled his struggling aircraft around and approached the runway. The concern on the faces of onlookers turned to horror as the Mustang suddenly swerved and exploded into flames. The unfortunate Captain Scholz was killed instantly.

Fifty years later (November 1993) a young woman was driving home along the B1052 road between Saffron Walden and Hadstock. As she reached the part of the road that once formed a section of the runway of the wartime airfield, she saw a flash of light and heard a siren. Thinking that a fire engine, police car or ambulance may be approaching, she slowed down and looked in her mirror. To her utter horror she saw an American Air Force pilot in full flying kit sitting on the back seat of her car. She skidded to a halt and nervously looked once again in her mirror, but this time the back seat was empty.

She sat in the car trying to regain her composure. Once she had calmed down a little, and convinced herself the car was now empty, she continued her journey home. A few days after the incident, while she was cleaning out her car, the young woman picked up a small object from the back seat. It was a button which was later identified as one from an American flying jacket. The woman, who had been familiar with the stretch of road, also remembered that after seeing the airman in her car she had stopped on a level with the old control tower of the airfield.

Another haunting associated with the old control tower is that of a young airman who was shot down during the First World War. Balls of flames have been seen on several occasions rolling down the runway as the ghostly pilot relives his untimely end in this residual haunting. Perhaps the most horrifying haunting associated with the old Hadstock aerodrome is that of a phantom American pilot who stands by the side of a road hitching a lift. This ghoulish apparition is said to have been an airman who was killed in a flying accident. Witnesses have been terrified by the sight of this apparition as he has no head.

The Witham Road Ghost

On the 10 February 2004 at 6.35 a.m., Steve Everett was driving along the B1389 road in Witham, towards Eastways Industrial Estate. It was a cold and clear morning and daylight was breaking.

As Steve approached the junction at the industrial estate he saw a man stood at the side of the road with a bicycle. Steve described the man as wearing a parker jacket, old trousers, a jumper and shoes. He also described him as 'rough looking'.

Steve was travelling at around 30 mph and as he approached the man he could see him looking up the road as if he were waiting for something or someone. As Steve drew level with the man, he walked straight out in front of Steve's car and vanished. Steve immediately stopped the vehicle and frantically searched for the man. He looked all around and under the car, but there was no sign of the man or his bicycle. As Steve told the website roadghosts.com at the time of the incident, 'I didn't believe in ghosts until I saw it yesterday. They think I'm mad at work, but there was something there.'

Looking back on the incident, Steve believed that the man was dressed in the style of clothes from the 1960s. Perhaps this spirit had originally lost his life on that stretch of road over fifty years ago.

The Spiderman of Stock

Charlie Marshall worked as an ostler in the village of Stock in Essex. He worked at the Bear Inn where he groomed the horses and slept in the stable loft. With a drinking habit and a shortage of money, Marshall decided to take advantage of the local legend about the Spider of Stock (*see* Mysterious Creatures section of this book). Marshall decided that he would become the Spiderman of Stock. At first he considered climbing the tower of the local church, but he could not obtain permission from the local clergy.

Marshall was not to be thwarted and took advantage of his residence at the Bear Inn. The Inn had huge fireplaces in each room and the chimneys were much larger than usual, so being a small and lithe man Marshall decided he would perform his Spiderman act at the Inn. He would get a pint of beer, climb up the chimney in one bar, sit in a little bacon loft up the chimney for a while and then come down the chimney in the bar next door when he'd finished the pint. Marshall would perform this feat up to twice a week for the local patrons, who would buy him beer and put money in his hat.

Sometimes they would play tricks on him and 'smoke him out'. On at least one occasion he was coming down a chimney when locals lit a fire and he had to turn around and climb back up the chimney, only to reappear in the other bar with a blackened face and angered expression.

One Christmas Eve Marshall climbed the chimney and failed to reappear. The locals rammed a bunch of faggots up the chimney and set fire to them. There was still no sign of him. The chimney was swept several times and there was still no sign of him. Marshall never came down alive. This wasn't the last time the Spiderman of Stock was seen though, as in time he began to haunt the Bear Inn.

Dick Weston, who was the landlord of the pub in the 1960s, claimed to have encountered the ghost of Charlie Marshall and said he liked him. Bob Stripe, who took over the pub after Dick Weston, also reported seeing the Spiderman. Other reported paranormal phenomena at the Inn include black footprints appearing on the carpets and strange falls of soot in the building. Over the years there have been several other sightings of Charlie Marshall at the

A depiction of the ghost of Charlie Marshall, seen on occasion hanging down from the chimney breast at the Bear Inn, Stock. (Illustration by Jason Day)

Bear Inn. On some occasions witnesses have claimed to see Charlie's face hanging down from the chimney breast.

The Phantom Bowler

During the 1940s, a man dressed in blue overalls was seen standing by a bench at lane seventeen of the Ambassador Bowling Club in Basildon. Customers would assume that the man worked at the bowling alley, until one time he simply vanished before their very eyes. The machinery of lane seventeen had a history of behaving erratically and there were also reports of temperature drops in that area – a common component of haunting phenomena. The Ambassador closed down in 1975 and was replaced with a ten-lane bowling alley called Basildon Bowl. Further reports of paranormal activity were reported at the venue too. It would appear that although lane seventeen was gone, the man in the blue overalls was still there. Basildon Bowl closed down in 1985 and Gala Bingo now occupies the building. Whether or not the man in the blue overalls still resides there is at this time unknown.

The Haunted Abbey

The Abbey at Waltham was the last in the country to be dissolved by Henry VIII in 1540. There had been a church on the site for hundreds of years, although the building had been rebuilt several times. The present building (the church of Holy Cross and St Lawrence), is the fourth on this site and was erected in the first quarter of the twelfth century, to replace the church founded by King Harold in 1060.

The church and grounds are said to be haunted by a girl who committed suicide in order to escape the unwanted attention of a man of the cloth. She is believed to be responsible for the

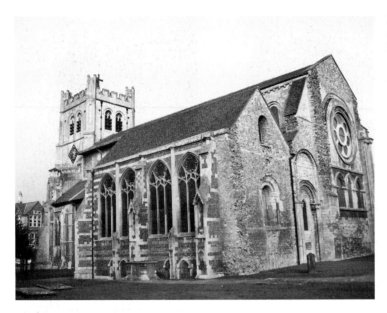

Mysterious lights and disembodied voices haunt Waltham Abbey. (Photograph by John Armagh)

sinister atmosphere in the building. An 'unearthly light' has been seen within the church on several occasions and the sound of plainchant has been heard, even when the building is empty at the time. Perhaps these phenomena are caused by the ghostly hooded figures seen walking regularly between the trees of nearby Monk Wood.

Secrets of the Nuclear Bunker

Kelvedon Hatch Secret Nuclear Bunker was built between 1952 and 1953, during the Cold War and was constructed on land requisitioned from the local farmer J.A. Parrish. The entrance to the bunker is situated deep into the woodland at Brentwood and is accessed via a mock bungalow. Beyond the blast screens inside is a 100ft-long tunnel and an amazing labyrinth of rooms built into a hillside, encased in 10ft thick reinforced concrete and 125ft underground. Initially the bunker was to be an RAF ROTOR Station, designed for up to 600 military and civilian personnel, possibly even the Prime Minister. Their collective task would be to organise the survival of the population in the awful aftermath of a nuclear war. The bunker then became a Civil Defence Centre during the 1960s and finally a Regional Government HQ.

The haunted tunnel inside Kelvedon Hatch Secret Nuclear Bunker. (Photograph by Kelly Day)

Right: The staircase between the three levels at Kelvedon Hatch Secret Nuclear Bunker. (Photograph by Kelly Day)

Below: An eerie looking mannequin inside the bunker at Kelvedon Hatch. (Photograph by Kelly Day)

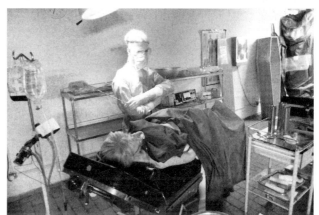

Above: The Medical Bay at Kelvedon Hatch, believed to be the most haunted room in the building. (Photograph by Kelly Day)

As the Cold War and the threat of nuclear attack died down, the bunker and its ancillary systems were no longer required by the government – it was costing up to £3 million a year to keep on standby. The bunker was decommissioned in 1992 and bought back from the government by the Parrish family, at a closed bid public auction. After forty years of secrecy, the bunker is now open to the public with a new lease of life as a museum, tourist attraction and events venue. Some would claim that not all of the areas of the bunker are completely revitalised, as many believe it is also home to the ghosts of the past.

The ghost of an RAF Officer has been seen moving from room to room, as has the grey figure of an unusually tall elderly lady. Witnesses have reported hearing footsteps, loud crashes and bangs that seem to have no explainable source. Unexplained lights and mists have also been reported in the bunker.

Several paranormal groups that have investigated the site believe that the medical bay is the most active and eerie area in the building. Dark figures have been seen in the room and there are even claims that an evil demonic entity resides in the sick bay too.

The Curse of John Francis

In May 1857, in Delhi, India unrest began. British officers had court-martialled eighty-five Indians from the Third Cavalry Regiment because they refused to handle the cartridges they had been issued. The major grievance with these cartridges was that they were greased with pig or cow fat, thus offending both the Moslem and Hindu Indian soldiers in the British army. The day after the arrest and conviction of these men, their fellow Indian soldiers mutinied and broke them out of their prison. They were soon to be joined by thousands more mutineers and the rebellion against the 'intensive ruling' of the British quickly spread across the whole of the country.

In June 1857, a terrible massacre occurred in Cawnpore, when surrendering British soldiers (under the leadership of General Wheeler), as well as women and children were killed. Many soldiers were shot by the rebels in full view of their families. The surviving men, along with the women and children, were to meet an even more horrific fate. Rebelling Indian Sepoy riflemen were ordered to hack the British to pieces, but they refused. Two butchers, two peasants and a bodyguard of Nan Sahib (an Indian rebel leader), carried out the heinous crime. Over two hundred men, women and children were butchered and their remains were thrown down a well. Among those killed was Terence Francis, a soldier from Brentwood, Essex.

In July 1857, Cawnpore was recaptured by the British under the command of General Havelock. The soldiers were quick to find evidence of the foul deeds of the rebels and one man in particular was determined to get to the bottom of things, quite literally.

John Francis was a British soldier serving with General Havelock in India and, knowing that his brother Terence had been serving under General Wheeler, he was determined to find him. John refused to believe that Terence had been slain and volunteered to take a party of men down the well to retrieve the remains of the victims. Piece by piece the bodies were brought to the surface, as thousands of bucketfuls of human remains were drawn from the well. As John Francis neared the bottom of the well he saw a human head that looked familiar. As he drew the head towards him with a wooden baton the head turned towards him and he let out an ear-splitting scream. The head belonged to his brother Terence. John was winched up, still cradling his brother's head, his own hair turning instantly white with shock. His comrades tried to take the macabre souvenir from him, only to be greeted by protesting shouts and a drawn pistol. Eventually, John fell asleep and Terence's head was taken from him and buried with the rest of the human remains from the well.

Following his ordeal John Francis was a shadow of his former self, returning to Brentwood to spend the last three months of his life a broken, bedridden man. Before his death he told friends how he was disgusted with the people of Brentwood and how little they cared about the plight of his brother and those in India. In his final words he uttered, 'If I can I'd like to come back and haunt them; they deserve a taste of the horrors that we went through for them. Damn it, I will come back and upset their pretty lives!'

So began the curse of John Francis.

In 1921 Doctor Walker was visiting a Brentwood pharmacist who put him up for the night. In the middle of the night, Walker was stirred from his sleep by a powerful, cold draft of air. As his eyes adjusted to the darkness he saw a shape at the bottom of his bed, from which he could pick out two faces. Walker called out and the figure stood up. As the form arose, Walker saw he was holding a human head. Walker passed out and hit his head on the bedpost, an injury that required hospital treatment. He then returned to London and put his experience down to dreaming, until he received a letter from a Brentwood school teacher relaying the story of John Francis to him.

There is an unusual amount of paranormal activity in Brentwood, particularly stories of haunted occurrences and poltergeist phenomena. Many of these incidents are, with some substance, attributed to the curse of John Francis.

The Seven Stars pub suffered poltergeist activity between 1951 and 1968. Reports from staff claimed that bottles were lifting from crates of their own accord and smashing on the cellar floor. The landlord himself claimed to have been pushed down the cellar stairs. Things got so bad that eventually nobody would work there. The pub closed down and became a bakery and offices.

During the 1960s another pub in Brentwood also experienced a poltergeist manifestation. Staff and patrons at The Fountain Head on Ingrave Road reported incidents including

furniture moving and beer bottles exploding in customer's hands. Around the same time, staff and guests at The White Hart Inn began witnessing similar phenomena. Taps began turning on and off by themselves and doors mysteriously locked and unlocked of their own accord. Household items went missing and then appeared elsewhere in the building and animals in the pub became agitated. The Swan Inn, also on Brentwood High Street, provided reports describing instances of strange knocking, windows and doors opening by themselves and an invisible presence that tapped customers and staff on the shoulder. Other pubs, such as the New World Inn and the Golden Fleece, were also experiencing unexplained occurrences, as were many private homes in the area.

Some people claimed that the ghosts of these Inns are former owners or customers, but there are others who believe it is the legacy of John Francis. There is one further incident where, much like that of Doctor Walker, the evidence points very firmly at a John Francis haunting.

In 1987 Donna Francis was walking past the Abbey National Building Society on Brentwood High Street, towards the White Hart Inn. As she walked past the building, she noticed a man's

A depiction of the ghost of John Francis holding the severed head of his brother. (Illustration by Jason Day)

reflection in the glass. The man looked as though he was behind her, but upon turning around she saw nobody there. Donna looked back in the window and the man's reflection was there again. He looked like he was holding something in his left hand which was down by his side. She looked more closely at the reflection and noticed that something was dripping onto the pavement from the object the man was holding. Again Donna turned around, but nobody was there. She looked down on the path beside her and what looked very much like a pool of blood had appeared from nowhere. The terrified woman ran into the White Hart pub and recounted her experience to the staff.

With nearly ninety years of paranormal activity so far, it would seem that the incredible curse of John Francis will not be lifted anytime soon.

The Spirits of Treasure Holt

On the site that now houses Treasure Holt, near Clacton-on-Sea, there has always been a building, going back as far as the early 1100s. The current construction, which is now known as Treasure Holt, dates back to 1138 and was formerly a farmhouse called Pearl's Farm. Previous to that it was a Coaching Inn. There are numerous stories and legends relating to this property that tell of witchcraft, murder and haunted incidents.

One such story claims that, when the building was an Inn, the landlord and landlady would ply wealthy travellers with drink. Once their guests were in a drunken stupor, they would help them upstairs to their room to sleep the drink off. The unfortunate souls would then be relieved of their money and valuables and murdered in their sleep. Their bodies were then dropped through a trapdoor and into a well. Although this is a story that has been passed down through time as legend, there may be some truth in it. In 1910 human bones were found under the floorboards in what is now the living room of Treasure Holt and in 1928, while a brick floor in the building was being re-laid, workers unearthed some leather buckles and more human bones.

The story continued that a monk named Simon travelled to the Inn with the intention of trying to curb the landlord and his wife's evil ways. Unfortunately, the monk is said to have fallen under their spell and become an accomplice of sorts. He purportedly died near what is now the driveway at Treasure Holt. This leads us to the first of five ghosts that are said to haunt the area. A monk has been witnessed walking about 1ft or so above the floor in the grounds of Treasure Holt. Indeed one of the owners of the property saw a dark, cloaked figure wander up the driveway as recently as the mid-2000s.

There have also been sightings of a woman dressed in a crinoline gown seen walking through the bedrooms in the house. A photograph taken from the outside of the building claims to have captured the woman's spectral image looking out through an upstairs window. On another occasion, the apparition of a blonde lady has been seen seated near the fireplace in the living room. Whether or not this was the same woman as the lady attired in crinoline remains a mystery.

Within the last decade the ghost of a young girl has been witnessed drifting through the bedrooms of the house. The owner of the house was woken by his wife, who saw a girl apparently sleepwalking. Believing it to be her daughter, she sent her husband to investigate.

He followed the girl through the darkened landing into his daughter's bedroom only to find that his daughter was in fact still fast asleep. Little is known of the spirit girl or why she has only recently made herself known to the occupants.

Perhaps one of Treasure Holt's most infamous phantoms is that of the ghostly cavalier. The cavalier has been seen many times around the building, wandering around in the lounge and also at the top of the stairs. On one occasion a man literally bumped into the cavalier on the stairs. After exclaiming at the apparition, the cavalier simply vanished before his eyes.

Treasure Holt's most prolific haunting began when visitors to the house recounted seeing the figure of a large red-bearded man in a grey suit appear at the window and walk across the living room and up the stairs. After posting the story in the local newspaper the identity of this spirit man was revealed. A woman contacted the owners of Treasure Holt and identified him as Uncle Percy. Percy lived in the house in 1917 and the numerous sightings of him since his death would suggest that he has resided there ever since.

Terror in the Tower

Layer Marney Tower is an impressive Tudor building situated near Colchester. Construction of the building was started by Lord Henry Marney, who died in 1523 before the project was finished. The building was passed on to his son who finished the building work. Following the second Lord Marney's death, there was no heir to inherit the building and so the estate passed into the hands of Sir Brian Tuke, the Treasurer to the Royal Household and Governor of the King's Posts. His daughter-in-law entertained Queen Elizabeth I there in 1579 and since then the house has passed into many different hands.

During the Great Earthquake of 1884 Layer Marney Tower was damaged considerably, but repair efforts ensued and the Tower was eventually restored to its former glory.

There are numerous ghosts associated with the estate, ranging from a Victorian lady who wanders the grounds as if searching for something to the shadowy figures that lurk in the old barn.

In the tower itself, it is said that phantom servants still perform their duties and are seen on a regular basis. It is not only apparitions that have been witnessed in the building; there are also reports of poltergeist activity.

Australian author Vivian Rae-Ellis recounted bizarre experiences during her two-year-stay at the tower. During her first night in the building she experienced a pressure on her chest and then felt the bed clothes being pulled as she tried to sleep. This activity continued for several nights until she discovered that if she left the bedroom doors open then nothing happened. Rae-Ellis believed that by leaving the doors open, the spirit could leave the room and wander the building freely. Other activity attributed to the poltergeist includes the slamming of doors. This has been witnessed by workmen in the building although, when they investigated the source of the commotion, they found that the only door in that area was rusted shut. Recently the poltergeist is said to be particularly active in the east wing of the building.

Layer Marney Tower's most dramatic and celebrated phantom is surely that of the ghostly knight on horseback. The nobleman, dressed in shining armour upon his magnificent steed, was not seen in the Tower's grounds, but incredibly, he was witnessed riding his horse down the 96 stairs of the spiral staircase. He is described as being adorned in full armour on his horse, appearing full of life, both with no transparency to them.

The Ghostly Soldier

Harwich Redoubt Fort was built between 1808 and 1810 to protect the port of Harwich against the threat of Napoleonic invasion. The building was constructed on a hill to allow for free views in all directions. To allow for this, a house was demolished and a large elm tree was also removed from the hill. During the two years it took to complete the work, it is said that French prisoners of war were made to help in the Fort's construction.

Once completed, the circular shaped Redoubt was 180ft in diameter, with a central parade ground which is 85ft in diameter. Originally armed with ten 24-pounder cannons, hoists were used to lift heavy shells from the lower level to the gun emplacements above. Between 1861 and 1862, work was carried out to accommodate a 68-pounder cannon, and the emplacements were strengthened (by adding granite facing) to withstand improved enemy artillery. Only a decade later in 1872, three of the emplacements were altered to take enormous 12 ton RML guns. In 1903, three emplacements received 12-pounder QF guns. Despite this ongoing modernization, the Redoubt never fired a shot in anger.

Due to the strategic importance of the fort declining in the 1920s, the Redoubt itself was allowed to fall into disrepair. The area around the building (previously kept clear to provide fields of fire) was bought by the Town Council and houses were built right up to the moat. With this, and the construction of the Beacon Hill Battery further along the coast, the Redoubt's fate was sealed.

Harwich Redoubt Fort, said to be haunted by a ghostly soldier.

The view from a gun emplacement, Harwich Redoubt Fort.

The fort enjoyed a short second spell in military service during the Second World War, when it served as a detention centre for British troops awaiting trial. Following the Second World War, the Redoubt was used by the British Civil Defence Authority and remained under their stewardship until it was disbanded and formally retired from military service.

The restoration of the Harwich Redoubt began in July 1969 and has continued until the present day. Currently open as a museum, the Redoubt is the largest ancient monument in the UK and is being restored by a voluntary group. In addition to some of the original guns that armed the Redoubt, there are a number of other guns on display. Around the parade ground on the lower level, the various rooms either present reconstructions of how they might have looked during their days in service, or are used to display other exhibitions.

With tales of paranormal activity coming from the fort, paranormal groups began investigating the building in the early 2000s. Witnesses reported seeing apparitions through windows and hearing unexplained footsteps. Visitors to the fort also testified to being physically touched by unseen hands in the lower casements. Other mysterious noises and hot and cold spots have been experienced by both staff and visitors alike.

Harwich Redoubt's most infamous apparition, the Headless Soldier, is often reported to be the instigator of these paranormal occurrences. It is reported that in 1872, when the big 12-ton cannons were being hauled into the fort, a hawser (hawser is a nautical term for a thick cable or rope) broke under the strain of the weight of the cannon. As the rope whipped back, it decapitated an unfortunate soldier standing nearby. There are differing descriptions of the apparition of this tragic soul who is said to have been seen in the fort. Sometimes he is reported to be seen headless and other times he is said to walk the grounds with his head tucked under his arm.

4
Big Cats

Big Cats (often called Alien Big Cats or ABCs) do not have anything to do with UFOs or visitors from other planets. The word 'alien' in this context simply means out of place. Big Cats are not cryptids or creatures unknown to science – they are simply animals that have been sighted in unexpected places. It is their location that is anomalous, rather than their existence. These creatures are also sometimes referred to as Phantom Cats, but the word 'phantom' is probably even more misleading than 'alien'.

Many people (including some researchers) believe that big cats originally began roaming the country as a result of animals being released or escaping from travelling menageries, which first appeared in Britain at the turn of the eighteenth century. In contrast to the aristocratic menageries, these travelling animal collections were run by showmen who met the craving of the ordinary population for sensationalism. Finding it hard to care for or feed a big cat, the average showman may just have simply let it go free. Alternatively, the animal could have been released as it simply did not attract the crowds anymore or because the showman went out of business and no longer needed it. Similarly, exotic animals were also believed to have been released into the wild in this country following the Dangerous Wild Animals Act coming into effect in 1976. Whatever the reason for them being there now, some big cats are believed to have adapted to their new habitats and bred offspring that have gone on to continue to breed offspring of their own. Eventually, we reach the present day and the big cats that are being spotted presently.

Such creatures have become synonymous with the County of Essex and sightings have been as varied as they have frequent. Animals such as black panthers, pumas and even the occasional lion have been encountered in the region. With names such as the Beast of Essex and the Fobbing Puma, sightings of these elusive animals become even more intriguing.

As with other phenomena in this book, listing every encounter with these creatures would be impossible, so here is a selection of the many sightings of the captivating big cats that roam Essex.

Early Big Cat Sightings

Regular big cat sightings in Essex are believed to have begun in the 1990s, but there are sightings that precede these. Two such reports appear to coincide with the Dangerous Wild

Animals Act coming into effect in 1976. Such reports appear to lend weight to the theory that the alien big cats of today are a product of animals being released into the wild following the legislation of 1976.

One of the first reported sightings of a big cat in Essex actually preceded the act itself by a month, when a large black cat was spotted in Pitsea in May 1976. Two years later, in April 1978, there were several sightings of an alien big cat in the general areas of Rochford and Hawkell. These reports were followed by several more throughout the 1980s and into the 1990s – and so the phenomenon of the Big Cats of Essex became renowned . Perhaps it was indeed this handful of cats, released in the 1970s, that were to be the forefathers of the animals that roam the county today.

The Colchester Big Cat

Over the past fourteen years a big cat has been seen roaming Colchester and the surrounding area. In 1996 there were at least two sightings of a large black cat, one along Mersea Road and another at Abberton reservoir. Sightings have continued throughout the nineties and into the millennium, from both rural and residential areas. Interestingly in October 2007 a man walking his dog saw the animal by the railway station, suggesting that big cats may now be venturing into more urban areas.

The Fobbing Puma

In 1978, drivers at the Lesney Matchbox Toy Factory near Fobbing became the first reported witnesses of a big cat that became known as the Fobbing Puma. The animal was 6ft long from nose to tail and had 'biscuit-coloured' smooth fur. The men reported the sighting to the police and claimed that the cat could definitely not been a mistaken identification of a dog.

Four years later another sighting occurred in Fobbing. In August 1982, at the Fobbing depot of the Essex Water Company, the hindquarters of a big cat were seen going into the undergrowth near the factory. As with the first sighting, the animal matched the description of a puma. The police were contacted and took the situation very seriously, alerting the public to look out for the puma. Days later, an individual walking on a foot path near the factory saw the creature cross the track in front of him. Upon investigation it was also noted that there was a strong smell of urine where the puma was seen. Again, the police were on the alert, as were farmers who were worried about their livestock.

A puma is believed to be on the loose in Fobbing.
(Photograph by Trisha Shears)

One theory about the Fobbing puma suggests that the sightings may have been linked with the terrain of the area. The location of the sightings was a flat and marshy region, used for industry. Andy Collins suggests that sightings near man-made areas of water, such as reservoirs and water towers, are the results of a disturbance of earth energies. Collins says that by creating large and unnatural expanses of water, a disturbance in the earth energies could trigger paranormal manifestations. If this is indeed the case, the suggestion is that the Fobbing puma may not have just been a big cat, but may have been some form of supernatural being or apparition.

The Beast of Essex

The Beast of Essex was first spotted lurking in the Braintree district in the mid-1990s. Since then, there have been more than eighty sightings around the county and this number continues to rise every year. Witnesses have described the beast as a 'giant black puma', but no such animal is known to science. Another description of the animal given by a witnesses, is that it is a 'black panther', which is a possibility.

One of the earlier sightings of the beast occurred in May 1996 near Cape Hill Golf Course in Braintree. Walkers there reported seeing a black cat in the area. Reports continued to flood in throughout the 1990s and by 2008, there were big cat reports regularly coming in from all over Essex. On 17 July 2008, a Ryan Air pilot spotted a black panther-like animal while travelling home from Stansted airport. The sighting occurred at 00.15 a.m. on Butler's Lane, between Saffron Walden and Ashdon. In August of the same year, another witness saw a similar creature in Brentwood. While sat in his car Mark Maylon saw a big cat sneaking along a hedgerow in a dark lane. He described the creature as 4ft long, 2 or 3ft tall and with a 2ft long tail. He observed the animal at a distance of 600 or 700 yards for a minute or two before it was out of sight. Just over two weeks later, the Beast of Essex was seen again on 15 September 2007. At 5.30 p.m. on Western Avenue in Epping, Roger Hart briefly glimpsed the animal for around ten seconds. He said, 'I was walking my dog down the lane from Western Avenue to the common when the cat crossed the path from one side to the other in front of me.'

The Beast of Essex is thought to be a wild panther. (Photograph by Bruce McAdam)

The following month, on the 7 November 2007, a similar animal was seen in Saffron Walden. The sighting happened at 5.55 p.m. on Bury water Lane. As the witness recalled:

I was walking my dogs, and the cat just stopped, then disappeared into a small copse. I have seen a very similar, if not the same, animal in the same area. I think it is a black panther that I have seen and heard. Too many normal people have seen similar animals, but are too afraid to go public for fear of being made to look a fool. I am not sure what to do about them as they do not appear to be doing any damage.

A further sighting, six days later, involved two witnesses. They were driving home at 11.30 p.m. on the 13 November, when they saw a big cat run into the bushes in a woodland area near Stansted Airport. The witnesses described the animal as jet-black, standing a metre tall, with green eyes and rounded ears.

One of the most recent and more interesting encounters with the beast occurred in the early hours of the morning on the 27 January 2009. An on-duty police officer saw the dark-coloured big cat as he headed back to base on Wivenhoe High Street. The unnamed officer said it growled at him before running off along the side of Wivenhoe police station.

A team of police officers were immediately dispatched to hunt for the creature when their colleague raised the alarm. They spent hours searching without success.

The Essex Lion

The year 1996 was a very interesting time for big cat sightings in Essex. Not only were panthers and pumas seen, but reports of a wild lion began being filed in the county. In January of that year in Tolleshunt Knights near Maldon, a witness reported seeing a creature they believed to be a lion wandering the small village. During the same month another sighting of a 'mountain lion' was filed five miles away in Great Wigborough, Colchester. Following these sightings the Essex Lion seemed to disappear – that is until twelve years later.

At 8.45 a.m. on the 25 January 2007, the lion was seen once again in the county. An eyewitness said, 'I was driving on the M11 and was one to two miles north of the Harlow turn off heading towards Cambridge, when a big cat, sandy in colour with dark patches, ran across the six lanes ignoring all traffic.'

The cat seemed unconcerned about the oncoming traffic as it maneuvered across the six lanes of the M11. The cat only glanced occasionally at some oncoming traffic before making it to the other side of the road.

After arriving home the witness called Essex police to see if there were any reports of a missing lion cub, or young lion from any zoos in the area. The witness described the animal as having front paws that 'dragged forward' and a long tail held up in a 'cat-like' fashion, looking very much like a lion cub.

The 'Essex Lion' has been sighted around the county since 1996. (Photograph by Trisha Shears)

Halstead Big Cats

The first sighting of an alien big cat in Halstead occurred in June 1996. A witness reported seeing a charcoal grey-coloured animal at close quarters. Ten years later, sightings of the cat still continue to be reported, including two very interesting encounters in 2007.

The first occurred on the 4 May, just off Morley Road in Halstead. A man let his dog out into his back garden, which is close to both an allotment and a graveyard, separated by a chain link fence. The dog became agitated by some thing on the other side of the fence, so the man walked over to have a look. The man saw an animal sitting between two trees in the undergrowth, approximately 25ft away. For roughly four minutes the man watched as the animal appeared to be watching him. It had two large pointed ears and he believed at the time that it may have been an injured fox. The man jumped the fence and approached the animal. As he got around 10ft away it jumped up and ran away to the right. From this clearer view the man described the creature as being a big cat. It was bigger than a domestic cat, with a large body and head, dark colouring, distinct ears and a long, thick tail. He called his wife and told her about the sighting and was surprised to hear that she had also seen the same cat in the last few weeks, but had not told him for fear of ridicule.

Another interesting account hails from a report of a sighting at Staple Field House in Halstead on the 14 July 2007. The eyewitness reported:

> I was riding my motorbike when the black animal figure jumped at me. It hit my exhaust. I think the animal fell to the ground because there is a lay mark in the corn field.

Reports of attacks on, or aggressiveness towards, people by big cats are very rare indeed, which makes this incident even more intriguing. With the two creatures encountered in 2007 reacting so very differently when confronted by human interaction, it may be possible that there is more than one big cat on the loose in Halstead. It remains to be seen whether the big cats of Halstead will be spotted again or indeed make another attack.

The Beast Of Ongar

In 1998 a secretive animal seen near Ongar was identified by experts on the BBC's wildlife series *X-Creatures*. They believed it was possibly a shy European lynx. This animal has become known to the residents of Essex, and big cat enthusiasts, as the Beast of Ongar. There have been several sightings of the animal over the last ten years, the most detailed of which occurred in the early 2000s.

In October 2003, an Essex woman described what she claimed was a sighting of the mysterious Beast of Ongar. She said she was quite convinced the animal was the same beast spotted years ago by others in the area. Kay Hayden, the clerk of the local parish council, told BBC Essex that she was shocked when a large black cat appeared in a field in Stanford Rivers, near Ongar off the A113. Ms Hayden said, 'All I can say is it was a great big leopard size. It was a muscular, completely black, strong looking animal, much, much larger than a dog.'

Four years later there was a spate of reports spanning several months in 2007. In March of that year Patrick Griggs, who lived next to Toot Hill Golf Club, began hearing strange noises while taking his dog for a late evening walk. Mr Griggs said, 'I haven't seen anything but I heard this extraordinary noise. It sounded like a cat but with a bass voice. It definitely wasn't a fox and definitely wasn't a dog. I called my wife and she heard the sound as well.'

A European lynx, one of which is believed to be the Beast of Ongar.

Later he found what he believed to be droppings from the big cat in his garden. Griggs continued, 'Just this week we've discovered some droppings in our garden of a size and form I've never seen before. They're in a prominent position, suggesting territorial marking which I believe is characteristic of big cats.'

A few weeks prior to Mr Griggs' account, a seven-year-old reported seeing a lynx as he was being driven home from school by his mother. The sighting happened opposite the Coopersale turn-off on the Epping-North Weald Road. The boy said that the cat came out of the wood into a clearing and stood and looked in the direction of the car as they drove past. The boy said the cat had a grey speckled body and pointy ears and was definitely a lynx. His mother said, 'Having an extreme interest in animals and wildlife and having numerous books on creatures, I've no doubt in him whatsoever. Although I did ask if he was sure it wasn't a deer or domestic cat, he remains adamant (it was a lynx).'

In May 2007 the Beast of Ongar was seen again. Stephen Monk said he saw a panther-like cat in fields at the bottom of his garden in Abridge after his dogs were alerted to something early in the morning. Monk was asleep on his sofa when his dogs began barking at the French doors. Mr Monk said:

It was like a panther – black with a long tail, about as big as my Labrador Mongrel dog, but not as fat. It would have been 3.5 to 4ft long and had a very long tail. At 4 a.m. in the morning it was like broad daylight. I half thought I wasn't believing what I was seeing. Had I been a bit quicker I could have grabbed my mobile phone and taken a picture of it. It ran right across the field about 60ft away from me.

Much like the Beast of Essex, the Beast of Ongar continues to be one of the most reported big cats in the county.

5

UFOs

Unexplained phenomena from the skies have been reported since man first looked up to the stars. As the years passed by, some believed that not all of these phenomena were natural occurrences with scientific explanations. Following a wave of sightings during the 1940s and 1950s, people began looking into this phenomena more closely. Science Fiction had become a popular genre in the media, both on the screen and in book form, and the suggestion that we may be being visited by alien beings in flying spaceships seemed to be a realistic possibility. The terms 'flying saucers' and 'UFOs' began being used to describe these sightings of aerial objects, which some believed were not attributable to known human technology. Another phrase that came into usage following the advancement of UFO research was the term 'close encounters'.

The term 'close encounter' refers to any interaction a witness may experience with a UFO or its occupants and any after effects following the encounter that may be attributed to that interaction. The UFO community, organizations and experts have set up a system to categorise these incidents into one of seven kinds of close encounter. Here is a brief description of the various types of close encounter.

Close encounter of the first kind – a sighting of one or more unidentified flying objects.

Close encounter of the second kind – an observation of a UFO and associated physical effects from the UFO, including heat or radiation, damage to terrain, crop circles, human paralysis, frightened animals, interference with engines, TV or radio reception and lost time (a gap in one's memory associated with a UFO encounter.)

Close encounter of the third kind – an observation of animate beings (who may be extraterrestrial or alien in origin) observed in association with a UFO sighting. This category would include all sightings of a being that is observed inside, outside or near a UFO. A close encounter of the third kind also includes cases where no entity or UFOs are observed, but the subject experiences some kind of intelligent communication.

Close Encounter of the fourth kind – a human is abducted by a UFO or its occupants. Some experts also include in this category non-abduction cases where absurd, hallucinatory or dream-like events are associated with UFO encounters.

Close encounter of the fifth kind – bilateral contact events that occur through the conscious, voluntary and proactive communication (human initiated or cooperative) with extraterrestrial intelligence.

Close encounter of the sixth kind – UFO incidents that cause direct injury or death. The difference between this category and the second kind is the severity of the physical effects suffered by the witness, which, as mentioned above, include death.

Close encounter of the seventh kind – human-alien hybridization. This concept also promotes the theory that extraterrestrials have perhaps interbred with and influenced ancient human beings in the past.

Essex has had more than its fair share of UFO sightings and close encounters over the years, with reports dating back to the early 1900s and continuing to the present day. It would be impossible to cover every reported UFO sighting from the county in this book, so here are just a few of the many UFO related incidents that have been reported in Essex.

The Original Southend UFO

One of the earliest UFO sightings recorded in Essex occurred on 5 September 1909. A London newspaper, the *Weekly Dispatch*, reported that residents of Southend had observed a luminous object crossing the night sky. Investigations revealed that a similar object was seen flying over Stanford about twenty minutes after the Southend UFO had disappeared.

The Pilot and the Flying Saucer

One of the most famous cases of a UFO sighting in Essex happened on 14 October 1954. Flight Lieutenant James Salandin was a pilot with the 604 County of Middlesex Squadron, Royal Auxiliary Air Force. Lieutenant Salandin had reported for duty at North Weald in Essex on the afternoon of the 4 October and took off in his Meteor Mark 8 jet at 4.15 p.m. As he headed south and gained altitude he observed two other Meteor jets flying above him leaving vapour trails. He checked his instruments and observed the movements of the other two aircraft in the cloudless sky above him. What Lieutenant Salandin thought was going to be a routine flight was just about to be become anything but that.

As Salandin was flying over Southend at 16,000ft, he suddenly spotted two circular objects coming from the opposite direction. They flew in between the other two aircraft and headed toward him. At first Salandin thought the objects were also airplanes, but then he noticed that they were not creating any vapour trails. He checked his instruments again and as the objects got closer, Salandin's initial surprise turned to horror. He explained:

A sketch of the view from James Salandin's cockpit during his UFO encounter. (Illustration by Jason Day)

When they got to within a certain distance, two of them went off to my port side, one gold and one silver. The third object came straight towards me and closed to within a few hundred yards, almost filling the windscreen. Then it went off toward my port side. It was saucer-shaped with a bun on top and a bun underneath, and was silvery and metallic. There were no portholes, flames, or anything. I tried to turn round to follow, but it had gone.

The flying saucer had miraculously avoided a last-minute head-on-collision with Lieutenant Salandin's Meteor jet by making an impossible high-speed manoeuvre. Although understandably shaken, Salandin flew around for a while to regain his composure and reported the incident by radio to ground control at North Weald. Upon landing, Salandin reported further details of the near miss to Derek Dempster, the 604's Intelligence Officer, who also became the editor of *Flying Saucer Review* a year later. A report was sent to the Air Ministry but nothing further was heard of the case until Dempsey printed an article about the incident in his magazine in 1955.

A footnote to the story is that Lieutenant Salandin did have an opportunity to capture some evidence of his UFO encounter. His Meteor jet had a gun camera fitted as standard, which was loaded and ready to take a picture at any time. Salandin explained that everything had happened so quickly, it was only after the incident that he realised his missed opportunity to gather some very valuable evidence indeed for the UFOlogists. This was something Salandin continued to regret as he pondered what he had encountered that afternoon. He concluded, 'I haven't found a satisfactory explanation for what I saw, but I know what I saw.'

The Langenhoe Incident

On Sunday, 14 September 1965, a twenty-nine year old man was returning to his home in West Mersea, after visiting his fiancée in Colchester. He was travelling at an average speed of 40mph on his motorcycle, overtaking a motor-scooter just south of Langenhoe. The sky was clear that night and the man recalled seeing the moon and stars overhead as he made his way home.

As he approached the road to Langenhoe Hall he heard a high-pitched humming. As the noise became louder he looked up to the sky, expecting to see an aircraft overhead. What he saw was not an airplane, but a small pinpoint of blue light to the east. The light was winking and rapidly became larger. It was then that the man realised it was heading in his direction from over Langenhoe marsh. The humming then changed pitched and turned into a buzz as it became increasingly louder. As it dawned on the witness that the light and the sound were connected, the engine of his motorbike coughed and spluttered, eventually stopping dead as its lights went out.

The blue flashing light was now only a mile away in the east and the man could decipher some sort of an outline. The large object then spun into view. He described it as resembling the upper half of a large spinning top. It appeared to be a dome on top with a strange flashing blue light inside. The object slowly descended, tilting as it moved. He was able to catch a glimpse of its underneath, which was rimmed by numerous round objects.

The witness dismounted from his motorcycle and approached the object. He became paralysed and was not able to move or speak. The witness recalled:

A motorcyclist witnesses a UFO in Langenhoe. (Illustration by Jason Day)

The flashing blue light became so intense that it was painful and it appeared to fluctuate in rhythm with my heart beat and hit against my chest. I felt myself tingling all over, rather like the electric shock one gets when handling an electrified cattle fence for too long. The buzzing then became quieter and the object descended in the area of Wick, where there are several farmhouses.

Suddenly, the scooter that the witness had overtaken on the road approached, its engine also coughed and suddenly stopped. The rider of the scooter, a young lad in a leather jacket, dismounted and stood petrified, staring at the blue light. He neither spoke nor looked in the witness's direction. With his head pounding and with a great effort the witness was able to move and grasped his motorcycle. As he pushed it along the road, he was relieved to hear the engine suddenly burst into life. He mounted the motorcycle and raced away from the scene as quickly as he could. As he raced down the road, the object was hidden by a tall line of hedges, but he could still see the blue glow in the sky for some time.

The witness arrived home at around 2 a.m. and woke his invalid mother. He was so terrified by his experience that he felt he must tell someone about it immediately. Two weeks later, Dr Bernard E. Finch interviewed the witness about his experience and, after cross-examination, he believed the witness's story to be 'true without doubt'.

The Aveley Abduction

At around 10 p.m. on 27 October 1974, a family of five (a young couple and their three children) were travelling home by car to Aveley, Essex. The couple noticed a strange blue light in the sky, which they at first thought was a helicopter. Within a short time they could make out the object was oval-shaped and pale blue in colour. They concluded that it must be some kind of UFO. Slightly unnerved, they headed along the B1335 (Sandy Lane) noting that the object seemed to be travelling in the same direction as their car. As they entered a bend in the road they encountered a strange green fog, which was about 9ft in height, covering the road completely. Having no other choice than to continue their journey, the father of the family drove through the disconcerting mist. As the car made its way through the fog its radio crackled as if being affected by some kind of static electricity, but scarily the radio was turned off. It then began to smoke and, fearing the risk of fire, the father pulled out the wires to the radio. The car seemed very cold and eerily silent as they passed through the fog, which according to the witness's claim may have only been for a second or two. The car emerged from the fog 'with a jolt', about half a mile further down the road and the family completed their journey home.

Upon reaching their destination the driver of the car rewired the radio as the rest of his family went inside the house. It was only then that his wife noticed the time. It was 1 a.m. and their journey should only have taken them twenty minutes. Instead of being home by 10.20 p.m. they now had nearly three hours of time they could not account for.

In an interesting side note Ufologist Andrew Collins, who learned about this case in August 1977, would later drive this very same route from Harold Hill to Aveley. It took him exactly twenty-two minutes to drive the nine miles distance.

Shortly after their UFO/fog encounter, the couple noticed three cars following them – a small red sports car, a blue jaguar and a large white car. All of which had darkened windows.

The couple also began having unusual, recurring dreams. Suspecting that these dreams might be masking real abduction memories or something of potential significance, UFO researcher Andrew Collins initiated the first steps to the couple being hypnotised. Their first session was set up for 25 September 1977.

During the regressions, the husband recalled being operated on by 'small ugly' beings that resembled 'gnomes'. He also remembered tests being carried out on him. His wife remembered an incident wherein she was laying on a flat wide table, feeling as if she could neither move nor speak, while a being of small stature in a white coat stood nearby. More details were to emerge with the subsequent hypnosis sessions that were carried out in October 1977.

The couple claimed to have been abducted and taken onboard the UFO that they saw on the night in 1974. Under hypnosis they recalled the car being hit by a white shaft of light through the green fog. The car was then transported up to the UFO as the couple blacked

A witness spots an unexplained light in the sky over Aveley from her car window. (Illustration by Jason Day)

out. Once they were inside the craft they became conscious and remembered seeing the car in a hanger 15ft below where they stood. They were then led by alien entities to separate rooms. They described encountering tall beings, about 6ft 6ins tall, with no visible mouths. A smaller being, which they identified as the 'examiner', was the one that 'operated the machine' and seemed to scan the husband's body. The husband also described what he was told about the ship's propulsion system. Apparently it was 'very complicated', but had something to do with 'ion-magnetic' energy and something called a 'vortex'. The couple claimed that they were examined and shown around the spacecraft, before being returned to their car and travelling along the road home again.

There is always conjecture when regression is brought into the equation. Scientists believe the simple fact that while under hypnosis people can be susceptible to suggestion, makes this a very unreliable way of acquiring information. Only the couple involved may ever know for sure if this was in fact a very real close encounter. However, never before had a case like this, where time had seemingly disappeared, been reported before in the UK and so the Aveley Abduction takes its place in UFO history.

Close Encounters at Hainault Forest

The bizarre incidents in Hainault began on 3 May 1977. Following a 999 call reporting an unidentified flying object in the vicinity of Hainault Forest, two uniformed police officers travelled to the scene. They arrived at around 4 a.m. and unlocked a gate to gain entry to the forest area itself. Once inside, the officers continued to drive through the park when they noticed a large red light in the sky, to the east side of the lake. They stopped their vehicle and got out of the car to observe the object more clearly.

The UFO was bell shaped and fairly low to the ground. The officers estimated that it was approximately 300 yards away from them and its size was a thumb nail held at arms length from their position. The object hovered in total silence and had a pulsating red light, going from dull to bright light and back again. The display occurred for two or three minutes before the craft suddenly disappeared from view. The police officers split up to approach the area where the object had been. No sooner had they began their advance on the position when one of the men spotted a white object in the sky above him. The object vanished almost immediately leaving a slight smell of burning in the air. The officers returned to their vehicle and reported the incident back to the police station via their radio.

Sketch of a 'Grey', the most frequently witnessed alien during a close encounter. (Illustration by Jason Day)

Three days later an even more unusual encounter was to occur in the forest. On 8 May 1977, two men were sat in their car in a marshy area of Hainault Forest. The men were waiting for the light rain to desist so that they could walk their dog. They decided to leave the car at around 7 p.m. and began walking their dog in the woods anyway, thinking that the dense woodland would protect them from the remaining drizzle. During their walk they heard a rustling sound in the bushes about 25ft in front of them. Suddenly a huge figure emerged from the bushes. The witnesses described it as being about 8ft tall, 4ft wide and dark blue in colour. The figure had no distinct arms or legs and appeared much brighter than its surroundings. The men watched the creature as it emerged from the bushes in front of them and disappeared into the woods on the other side of the path. The startled witnesses recounted their story to an investigator who was near the forest at the time, investigating the UFO report from 5 May.

As yet there is no conclusive proof that the two sightings are related but, due to the close proximity of the incidents, it is a possibility that the blue creature sighted in the forest could have arrived in the craft spotted by the policemen three days earlier. The question is, will either be seen there again?

The Blackmore Heptagon

A nightclub manager briefly witnessed a sight that completely confounded him in 1985. At 7.05 p.m. in the skies above Blackmore (near Stansted), the man saw what he described as a UFO that was shaped like a fifty pence piece.

The object was observed for around five minutes, in which time the hovering, heptagon-shaped craft was seen to project two beams of light from the front and two weaker beams from its rear. The witness also noticed that the vessel had red, yellow and green clusters of light on its underside. The UFO then moved away at speed before vanishing from sight.

The Brentwood Discs

Between 10.30 p.m. and 11.10 p.m. on Thursday, 28 May 2009, a father and daughter from Brentwood witnessed UFO activity in the sky from their back garden. Two red, disc-shaped objects were observed pulsating silently in the sky. The objects then took off at high speed in the direction of Romford. Just as the father and daughter thought their encounter was over, they spotted the discs again, only this time there were four or five of them. The craft were flying in formation above each other and then switched to a horizontal straight line formation. The daughter was using binoculars to observe the craft and also noted that she could see green lights on the vessels. The sighting lasted a total of forty minutes before the UFOs vanished.

The Canvey Fireball

In 2009, five people observed what they believed to be a UFO in the skies above Canvey Island. At 10.45 p.m. on Saturday 13 June a man was standing in his garden smoking a cigarette

Depiction of the 'fireball' seen over Canvey Island in 2009.
(Illustration by Jason Day)

when he noticed something conspicuous overhead. What he saw was an orangey-red looking ball silently crossing the sky. He believed it resembled something of a 'fireball' and had 'lines' coming from it. The witness was joined by his wife and three other witnesses and managed to take photographs of the UFO before it disappeared. One of the witnesses noted at the time, 'Although planes go across this area sometimes in an evening, there was a noticeable lack of noise and flashing lights during the sighting.'

The Braintree Lights

On Sunday, 30 August 2009, a couple were travelling along the A120 towards Braintree, when they saw something very curious in the sky. Just as the junction for Braintree town was coming up they saw nine orange lights in the sky. According to the witnesses the lights were not bright and appeared to have 'ragged edges'. As they drove towards the lights they split into two groups on either side of the carriageway. Intrigued, the couple turned their car around and went back to check, but the lights had gone. The only lights they could see in the sky were aircraft lights.

What the lights were is still unexplained. Was it something as straightforward as Chinese lanterns or could it have been a squadron of UFOs?

6

Witchcraft, Mediums, Healers and Miracles

Witchcraft, in various historical, religious and mythological contexts, is the alleged use of supernatural or magical powers, usually to inflict harm or damage upon members of a community or their property. Other uses of the term distinguish between bad witchcraft and good witchcraft (Black Witches and White Witches), with the latter often involving healing, perhaps remedying bad witchcraft. Essex has a long history of paganism and witchcraft, most notably with the Essex Witch Trials and the Canewdon Coven.

Another paranormal phenomena associated with witchcraft is that of Medicine Men, also known as Cunning Men, wizards or healers. These men were said to cure ailments or break evil curses by using herbal remedies or casting spells. Again, Essex has an association with such men through the work of James Murrell and George Pickingill.

It is said that healing can also be achieved by divine intervention or, to put it another way, by a miracle occurring. A miracle is an unexpected event attributed to God. Sometimes an event is also attributed (in part) to a miracle worker, saint, or religious leader. The story of Saint Osyth of Essex is one such alleged example.

Mediumship is the claimed ability of a person (the medium) to experience contact with spirits of the dead, angels, demons or other immaterial entities. The role of the medium is to facilitate communication with spirits who have messages to share with non-mediums. Mediums claim to be able to listen to, relay messages from, and relate conversations with spirits. Mediumship is also part of the belief system of some New Age groups including the Spiritualist Movement. It is also an integral part of the teachings of the Arthur Findlay College in Stansted.

This section deals with all of the aforementioned cases and more, as we delve deeper into the world of witchcraft, mediums, healers and miracles in Essex.

The Six Witches of Canewdon

The village of Canewdon near Southend-on-Sea has a long history of association with witchcraft. Legend has it that this dark history began when the Canewdon coven of witches was founded in the fifteenth century by a local landowner, who fought in France and had there been initiated into 'the craft'. It was believed that there would be six witches living in the village ('three in silk and three in cotton'), as long as the tower at St Nicholas' Church stood.

Rumour had it that at one time, one of the witches was the wife of a local clergyman. Every time a stone fell from the 75ft tall church tower, it was said a witch would die and another would take her place in the coven.

The first documented instance of witchcraft in Canewdon dates back from the sixteenth century when a local spinster, Rose Pye, was accused of bewitching a child to death. Rose was later acquitted of the charge at the assizes in July 1580. By the early nineteenth century, the village had become synonymous with stories of the supernatural. The church, dedicated to St Nicholas, became linked with magic, witchcraft and the devil and unholy ceremonies were said to have been performed within its sacred grounds.

During the 1800s the Canewdon witches were said to have terrorised the village. They allegedly inflicted plagues of lice and other parasites upon their enemies, inflicted minor illnesses on the local population and even cast spells on wagons so their wheels would not turn. Most of these alleged witches were old women who lived alone and kept white mice as pets. These were regarded as imps or familiar spirits in animal form and had to be passed on when the witch made her final journey to the spirit world, although sometimes they were buried with their mistresses. Every Coven of witches was believed to be under the control of a male wizard, who was known as the Master of the Witches and the Canewdon witches were no different.

The village sign at Canewdon includes a depiction of a witch. (Photograph by Terry Joyce)

In the late nineteenth century the Master of the Witches in Canewdon was a farm labourer George Pickingill or Pickingale (the family name was spelt both ways), who lived in an old cottage near The Anchor pub, a few hundred yards form the church. Pickingill was known as a cunning man whose skills included divining and using charms for healing purposes. He also had a sinister side to his image. The village locals recounted tales of Pickingill stopping farm machinery with a stare from his intense blue eyes and cursing those who offended him with his blackthorn walking stick. Pickingill died in 1909 and was buried in an old part of the churchyard. On the day of his funeral, as the horse drawn hearse drew up at the church gate, the animal escaped its harness and cantered off up the lane.

It was said that his imps haunted his empty cottage for many years and passers-by reported seeing their red eyes glowing in the darkness until it was eventually demolished. It is claimed that shortly before his death Pickingill disbanded the Canewdon coven. Persistent rumours, however, suggest that the craft is still flourishing underground in the area and that remnants of the Coven were still active elsewhere.

In a wood near Canewdon , shortly after Halloween 1975, a pin-studded doll was found next to a black candle, which revived belief in the village that the witches were still active. On a country lane, during the 1980s, locals reported seeing a man on a motorcycle being chased by a small demonic entity. The creature was said to have been as fast as the motorbike. In more recent years, there have even been reports detailing the ghost of an old witch materialising out of a grey mist by the church gate. She is said to emerge from the churchyard and rise a couple

An early illustration of witches and their familiars.

of feet into the air before rapidly moving towards the river. She is said to be clad in crinoline with a large poke bonnet. The most alarming feature of this spectre is that beneath her bonnet she is said to have no head. Perhaps then, at least one of the Witches of Canewdon may still frequent the village in some shape or form.

The Miracles of St Osyth

The village of St Osyth is in north-east of Essex and derives its name from a seventh-century Anglian Queen and saint. Osyth's story is one of murder, miracles, life after death and the paranormal.

Osyth was born into royalty. Her father, Redwald, was the first Christian King of East Anglia. Wilburge, her mother, was daughter to the King of the Mercians. As a small child, Princess Osyth was sent to be educated by her Aunt, St Edith, an abbess in charge of a nunnery at Aylesbury. One day Edith sent Osyth on an errand to take a book to St Modwenna. In order to reach Modwenna's house, Osyth had to cross a bridge that spanned a stream. There had been a recent flood causing the stream to swell and there were strong winds too, so crossing the bridge was a treacherous task on this occasion. As Osyth began to take her first steps onto the bridge, a strong gust of wind swept her into the icy cold waters of the stream.

When Osyth failed to return, Edith went to visit Modwenna and realised the child was missing. The two women scoured the countryside to no avail. Undeterred, they continued their search for three days, until finally they found the lifeless body of Osyth lying in the stream where she had tragically drowned. St Modwenna began praying for Osyth and was quickly joined by Edith. Modwenna then commanded Osyth to rise from the water by the power of God and, unbelievably, that is exactly what she did. Miraculously, Osyth came back from the dead.

With her life changed forever by this experience, Osyth decided to dedicate her life to the church and made it her vocation to become a nun. Osyth's parents did not share her vision and, with a view to forming an alliance with the East Saxons, betrothed her to King Sibere. Osyth never gave up on her quest to keep her vow and despite going through with the marriage she knew one day she would be an abbess. While her husband was away on a hunting trip she took the opportunity to slip away and become a nun.

After the initial grief and anguish of his wife's departure, Sibere generously gave her land to build a nunnery and a church ten miles south-east from Colchester. Here, Osyth set about her godly duties and was able to carry out her vow for a number of years, until one fateful day in autumn.

This was a period in history when it was common for Danish invaders to carry out raids up and down the English coast. They would plunder monasteries, burn villages and attack the local people. These attacks predate the actual Viking settlers – this was a time when the pirates would carry out their crimes and return to their native country with their haul.

In October AD 653, Osyth was walking in the nearby woods (now known as Nun's Wood) when she was confronted by such a marauding gang of Viking pirates. She came face-to-face with the Viking leader in a clearing within the woods. The pagan leader insisted she renounce her Christian faith and also her virtue. Osyth stood her ground and refused, despite the threats of the gang. With no respect for the pleas of the abbess, or her Christian beliefs, the Viking leader wielded his glinting sword and beheaded Osyth with a single blow. The Vikings stood

St Osyth carries her severed head towards the village church. (Illustration by Jason Day)

in disbelief and astonishment as Osyth stood up, bent down and picked up her own head. Holding it at arms length and guided by angels, she proceeded to walk to the village church. She knocked loudly on the door with her bloodstained hand to warn the nuns within of the approaching Vikings, then slumped to the ground and died.

At the place of her martyrdom in the woods, a spring gushed forth. The spring became a stream and a well was built in her honour. This became known as St Osyth's sacred well. The spring water in the well is said to possess special, miraculous properties and has been used to bless people, who often claim that it has cured their ailments.

The centre of the present day village of St Osyth is dominated by the medieval remains of a priory set in 383 acres of land and built in her honour. The building of the priory began in the year 1118 and was established for the Augustine Canons. It became one of the great Augustine Abbeys of Europe. The gatehouse of the priory still stands today and is one of the many locations at which St Osyth's ghost has been seen. One witness reported seeing the ghost of a woman standing by a washing machine while the building was being used as a nursing home

Legend has it that Saint Osyth herself haunts the building and manifests there every year on 7 October. Her spirit is said to walk the priory walls, still carrying her severed head in her hands. St Osyth has also been spotted in Nun's Woods and in the local churchyard.

Other witnesses have reported seeing a pale monk walking around the priory at night carrying a candle, while several other people claimed to have watched a procession of monks walk by a window.

An aerial view of St Osyth Priory Church. (Photograph by Terry Joyce)

Matthew Hopkins, the Witchfinder General

Matthew Hopkins was born in 1620 and was the youngest son of James Hopkins. James was a Puritan Minister and lived in Great Wenham in Suffolk, England. Little is known of Matthew Hopkins' childhood, though it is thought that he would have been educated at a grammar school and, without a doubt, he would have been instructed in the righteous preaching of the Puritan cause from his father. Matthew did not go onto University as his father and brothers had. The fact that his signature appears on a conveyance from 1641 suggests that he was an apprentice to, and later became, a lawyer. By 1644 Hopkins had moved across the River Stour to Manningtree, Essex. During this time England, and in particular Essex, was in the grip of 'witch fever'. Following the witchcraft laws of 1542, 1563 and 1604, the death penalty was liable for, 'Invoking evil spirits and using witchcraft, charms or sorcery whereby any person shall happen to be killed or destroyed.'

Hopkins began his career as the self-styled Witchfinder General in March 1645. He joined John Stearne, both having been authorised by the magistrates to investigate a suspected witch. The suspect, Elizabeth Clarke, was alleged to have brought about the cause of a convulsive illness and death of a local tailor's wife through witchcraft. Hopkins' primary tool in his investigation was to use sleep deprivation. After three days and nights of this torture, Elizabeth Clarke confessed. The one-legged widow admitted, in front of witnesses, to summoning beasts that were familiar spirits, which she used to harm others. She confessed that the devil was their father and also divulged the names of other witches in Manningtree. Her confession led to the exposure of a coven, which Hopkins claimed had sent a spirit to kill him.

Hopkins and Stearne travelled the length and breadth of Essex in search of witches. They employed the help of midwives and Witch Prickers in their efforts to gather evidence and persuade a jury. The midwives, also known as search women, would identify the genital teats where imps were supposed to suckle on the alleged witch. Anne Leech, a widow from Mistley in Essex, was examined by one of the search women. She admitted several offences after marks were found 'around the privie parts of her body'. 'Witch pricking' was the method of pricking a suspects 'witch mark' with a knife. If the witch mark did not bleed then this was said to prove the guilt of the accused.

In July 1645 twenty-nine women, who had been held in a dungeon in Colchester Castle on suspicion of practicing witchcraft, were moved to Chelmsford to face trial. Hopkins had persuaded Rebecca Lawford, who was charged with causing a woman to miscarry, to turn Crown evidence against several others to escape the noose herself. Hopkins and Stearne moved on to Suffolk to continue their witch finding crusade, but returned to give evidence in the trials and were witnesses against many of the accused. The women were tried by the Earl of Warwick, who was not a professional judge but in fact a Puritan Soldier. At the end of the trials one woman was acquitted and another nine were reprieved due to insubstantial evidence. The nine women were remanded in gaol until their pardon applications were sent to parliament; at least one of them died while waiting. The nineteen remaining women were to be hanged. English witches were not burned at the stake as they were in the continent. Death at the stake was reserved as punishment for traitors and heretics, under the Witchcraft Act of 1563. Death by hanging was the sentence carried out on those found guilty of sorcery. Four of the women were hanged at Manningtree and the other fifteen women met the same fate at Chelmsford. Margaret Moone collapsed and died on her way to the gallows. She had proclaimed on several occasions that the Devil often told her she would never be hanged. Elizabeth Clarke, the first woman accused of witchcraft by Matthew Hopkins, was helped to a height where the noose could be put around her neck (because of her disability) and then hanged.

Matthew Hopkins, the Witchfinder General.

Above: A prison cell at Colchester Castle, used to hold women accused of witchcraft during the Essex Witch Trials. (Photograph by Kelly Day)

Right: Another view of one of the prison cells at Colchester Castle. (Photograph by Kelly Day)

Hopkins and Stearne went their separate ways once they had embarked on their crusade of Suffolk. Hopkins took the east side and Stearne took the west. By now, Hopkins was enjoying the power and material wealth that being a Witchfinder afforded him. He employed two assistants, wore fashionable Puritan clothing and was earning £15 to £23 per town cleansed of witches – that being at a time when wages were as little as 12.5*d* per week. Hopkins and Stearne had earlier faced a stand off with the townsfolk in Colchester during the witch trials in Essex. It would seem that the people of Suffolk were growing concerned with Hopkins' allegations and methods during his investigations in their county. Rumours were beginning to circulate that he was manipulating confessions from elderly, defenceless women with pets. One example of this was a woman from Suffolk:

> Faith Mills, of Fressingham, Suffolk, admitted that her three pet birds, Tom, Robert and John, were in reality familiars who had wrought havoc by magically making a cow jump over a sty and breaking a cart. She was hanged.

Hopkins was also rumoured to be using a retractable blade during 'witch pricking'. If this were the case, Hopkins could construe a guilty conclusion on the suspected witch every time the test was carried out. Opposition to Hopkins' bloody persecutions had grown and the end was near for the Witchfinder General.

In 1646 a parishioner showed John Gaule, the Puritan Minister of Great Staughton, a letter written by Matthew Hopkins. The letter asked if he would be welcome in the parish.

Hanging was the punishment for witchcraft and Matthew Hopkins sent many an accused woman to their death. (Illustration by Jason Day)

The Ducking Ponds, where accused witches would be plunged into, at Mistley Place. (Photograph by Kelly Day)

Gaule replied by preaching against Hopkins from the pulpit and hinted that Hopkins himself was a witch. Gaule also published a book called *Select Cases Of Conscience Touching Witches and Witchcraft*, an expose of Hopkins' methods, which condemned him and Stearne. Gaule's preaching added to complaints already made against Hopkins and forced him to answer some awkward questions before judges in Norwich. Hopkins protested, saying he was the victim of rumours and conjecture. He was also, by this time, suffering from an illness believed to be consumption.

Meanwhile, John Stearne had continued onto the Isle of Ely and Cambridgeshire, but the damage was already done by John Gaule's campaign against the witchfinders. Public opinion was going against them and after the witch trials in Ely acquitted the accused witches, Stearne retired. He later wrote a memoir published in 1648 entitled *A Conformation and Discovery of Witchcraft*, in which he exonerated both himself and Matthew Hopkins of any wrongdoing. By the end of the East-Anglian witch craze, as many as 300 people are believed to have been accused and over 100 were executed. In Suffolk alone Hopkins is believed to have had sixty-eight people executed.

So what became of the Witchfinder General? There is a tradition that Hopkins was subjected to his own swimming test. After returning from Suffolk to his home in Mannigntree, Hopkins endured the test at the hands of disgruntled villagers and, because he floated rather than drowned, he was hanged for witchcraft himself. Most historians believe, however, that Matthew Hopkins died of tuberculosis in his bed shortly before the retirement of his partner John Stearne in the autumn of 1647. The parish records for Manningtree in Essex record Hopkins' burial in August 1647. Some people believe that Hopkins was buried at Mistley Heath, which is now an overgrown field. Other historians believe that his final resting place is in Mistley Place Woods by the Hopping Bridge in Mistley. However, neither Mistley Heath nor Mistley Place seem to be the final resting place of Matthew Hopkins. For the reported sightings of his ghost in various locations in both Mistley and Mannningtree would suggest that Hopkins, and at least one of the women that he condemned to death, are not resting anywhere.

At Mistley Place a ghost, reported to be the spirit of Matthew Hopkins, has been encountered around the Ducking Ponds (used during the witch hunts) and the woods at what used to be Hopkins' headquarters, by visitors and paranormal investigators. At the nearby Hopping Bridge in Mistley a 'phantom jaywalker' is also reported to be the ghost of Matthew Hopkins. He has been seen wearing seventeenth-century clothing and walking in the vicinity of the small hump-backed bridge.

During his lifetime Matthew Hopkins is said to have frequented the White Hart Inn, Manningtree and it is reputed his spirit can still be heard in the building to this day.

Mistley Place Woods, said to be the final resting place of Matthew Hopkins and allegedly haunted by both Hopkins and also many of his victims. (Photograph by Kelly Day)

The Thorn Hotel in Mistley is also said to be visited by the ghost of Matthew Hopkins. A phantom serving-girl, who used to work at the hotel, is alleged to still walk along the corridors and a boy, who was pushed under a cart and trampled to death during a fight, is seen at the rear of the building. Another haunted Inn associated with the spirit of the Witchfinder General is the Red Lion in Manningtree. This pub is said to be haunted by a Victorian gentleman nicknamed George, although many people claim the ghost is actually that of Matthew Hopkins.

Reports of the ghostly screams of a tormented witch being interrogated at the hands of Matthew Hopkins, are said to be heard coming from the opposite shore from the River Stour in Manningtree. The ghost of Elizabeth Clarke, executed on the orders of Hopkins, is said to walk the shoreline of Seafield Bay. Sounds heard here on certain nights have been attributed to the cries of tortured witches and also the sound of Elizabeth Clarke's familiars looking for her.

The last English witch was executed in 1685. The final conviction for witchcraft occurred in 1712 and the Witchcraft Act itself was repealed in 1736.

Is the ghost of Matthew Hopkins still looking to rid the country of witches from beyond the grave? Or is the legacy of the Witchfinder General buried with him in a field in Mistley?

The Psychic School of Arthur Findlay

Arthur Findlay is a name synonymous with the world of spiritualism and mediumship. Arthur was born in 1883 and by the age of seventeen, he had developed an interest in the field of comparative religion. Findlay became an accountant, stockbroker and magistrate and by 1913 had been awarded the Order of the British Empire for his work with the Red Cross during the First World War. His extensive research into religion and beliefs continued throughout this period. By 1919, Findlay had become a believer and practitioner of spiritualism and a year later he founded the Glasgow Society for Psychical Research. Much of this interest and belief in the paranormal came from an encounter with a Scottish medium called John Sloan. Sloan claimed he was able to communicate with spirits through the practice of 'direct voice communication' – where the spirit uses the medium's vocal chords to convey their messages. Findlay studied Sloan's abilities for five years and produced several volumes of his findings in book form.

His interest in paranormal phenomena increased, and by 1920 he had founded the Glasgow Society for Psychical Research. In 1923 Findlay took part in the Church of Scotland's inquiry into psychic phenomenon. In the same year, he retired from his professional business and purchased Stansted Hall in Essex, a manor house built in 1871. Findlay had now devoted his life to spiritualism and in 1932 he became a founding member of *Psychic News*, a Spiritualist newspaper, along with Hannen Swaffer and Maurice Barbanell.

Findlay first mooted the idea of a Spiritualist College at Stansted to the Spiritualists' National Union in 1945 (an organization that Findlay himself would become an honorary president of). After personal contacts with three successive Union Presidents, a will was drawn up and in 1954 the National Council accepted the proposed bequest of Stansted Hall with an endowment. This was followed by a later gift in the form of stock, to be used for furnishing and decorating. In 1964, a year after the death of his wife, Mr Findlay transferred the Hall, grounds and endowment to the Union. Arthur Findlay himself died in July 1964.

Findlay's vision of a Spiritual College had become a reality. Holding over sixty courses every year, the Arthur Findlay College (formerly Stansted Hall) is now a residential centre, where students can study Spiritualist philosophy, healing, mediumship and psychic abilities. Courses, lectures and demonstrations are all offered by leading exponents and, with the additional features of a library and museum as well, Stansted Hall is considered the world's leading facility for the advancement of Psychic Science.

The Witch that Followed

Terry Palmer, a writer and publisher, set off to find the resting place of the last witch in England to be burned at the stake. Little did he know that the spirit he sought would be accompanying him on his journey.

The spirit in question was allegedly called Elsa and, depending on the version of the story you chose to believe, she was either burned at the stake on the old village green of Dedham in 1763, or hanged in 1763. Whichever the case may be, while researching his book *Spook in the Well*, Terry set out to find her. Early in his quest, Terry attended a séance and Elsa herself came through and claimed she would be with Terry for all time, no matter where he went. It was then that inexplicable things began to happen around him.

He visited a former convent and a dog ran out, barking and wagging its tail at him. The dog then ran back to its master before running back toward Terry barking and leaping into an empty space behind him. Just a few days later, while visiting a shop, another dog barked at Terry and then at the empty space behind him. Terry began to believe that Elsa's spirit had in fact possessed him.

Finally Terry claimed to have found Elsa's grave near an Inn not far from the village where she was executed. He stood on the spot and felt a tingling throughout his entire body. Terry and a friend dug up the location, but found no remains. Legend has it that following her murder, Elsa's body was in fact thrown down the well at the Inn and her ghost is said to now haunt the building.

Elsa is seen in full skirts on the staircase between the two bars at The Sun Inn at Dedham. On one occasion she appeared dressed in a brown skirt, sitting on the staircase and weeping. Her ghost is said to be seen at midday, and only midday. Some reports say that her ghost is only visible to women.

Cunning Man Murrell

In the 1800s there were several men in England that held the moniker Cunning Man. A Cunning Man was regarded as a wise man, a healer, or put in simple terms a kind of Christian Witch Doctor. The greatest Cunning Man in all of England was James Murrell. Murrell was famed for his healing powers, clairvoyance, herbal remedies, divining, astrology, casting and spell breaking.

Cunning Murrell was born in 1790 in Rochford, Essex and was the 'seventh son of a seventh son'. This sign marked him for a life of magical empowerment. Murrell worked as a surveyor's apprentice before moving to London to become a Chemist's assistant, a job that no doubt helped him with his herbal remedies later in life. He returned to Essex and settled in the village of Hadleigh around 1812. Murrell rented a small cottage facing Hadleigh Church, from where he became a cobbler, making shoes for the local people.

Murrell eventually gave up shoemaking and became full-time herbalist, healer and seer. His reputation as a Cunning Man had spread far and wide and people came from all over the country to seek his advice. Not only was he visited by ordinary folk, but also by wealthy and aristocratic people. Murrell held his consultations in the living room of his cottage. The room was filled with magical textbooks, a knife, hanging herbs and a skull. There were also chairs, a desk and a large brass telescope, all the tools of his trade. One such tool Murrell had at his disposal was a magical mirror. He would use this in his capacity as a seer, for divination purposes and to find lost or stolen property. On other occasions he would use a bowl of water that had a black ink spread on the surface. Many who consulted Murrell claimed they saw events that happened miles away in the bowl. He would also wear a copper bracelet on his wrist, which he claimed had the power to detect dishonest men. His predictions as an astrologer were uncommonly accurate and he was said to be able to predict events that were many years into the future. Murrell's magical telescope was said to show future events, but apparently it could also see through walls.

His healing powers were also beyond compare and he was said to be able to cure animals of ailments by simply laying his hands on them. Murrell would also use witch bottles to break a curse or a spell inflicted on somebody by another witch. These bottles would be filled with specimens taken from the victim, such as nail clippings, blood, hair and urine, to which he would add other ingredients.

One case that came to Murrell's attention was a young woman who was cursed by a gypsy. The girl was made to bark like a dog and came to Murrell for a cure. He quickly diagnosed witchcraft as the cause of her ailment and prepared a witch bottle to cure her. Murrell heated the bottle on his cottage stove to send out the sensation of burning to the gypsy and compel her to remove the curse. Unfortunately, Murrell left the bottle on the stove too long and it exploded. The following morning the badly burned body of a gypsy woman was found dead in a lane in the village. The curse was broken and the young woman was cured.

James Murrell was often referred to as the 'Master of Witches' and indeed he himself believed that he could force any witch to do his bidding. He also believed he could invoke the spirits of elementals to aid him too. That said, Murrell was in fact an extremely religious man and could recite the bible backwards. He also believed he could induce angelic spirits to aid him in his work. This mixture of good and evil often caused him to be involved in many arguments with the local clergy, but Murrell at least had a cordial relationship with the local vicar.

In December 1860 Murrell became ill. He called for a pen and paper and, foreseeing his own death, calculated the day of his passing. Murrell was once again correct in his prediction and he died on 16 December 1860. During his final hours, the village vicar tried to minister the last rites to him. Murrell fixed his eyes on him and shouted, 'I am the Devil's master.'

The vicar ran from the room in fear. Despite this outburst, James Murrell was given a proper burial in an unmarked grave in Hadleigh Churchyard.

7

Unexplained Phenomena

Extraordinary rainfalls, mysterious patterns appearing in crops and vehicles rolling uphill – these are just some of the mysteries that come in the category of Unexplained Phenomena. Others include bizarre human conditions that remain unsolved by science, such as people being in two places at once or bursting into flames. There are also stories of time slips and encounters with apparitions in crisis, all of which fall into the paranormal category.

These unexplained phenomena have occurred on more than one occasion in the county of Essex. In this section you will discover more about these bizarre occurrences.

A Rain of Straw

Throughout history there have been many instances of strange things falling from the sky. These include falls of fish, ice, frogs and even coins. One such case of 'paranormal rain' occurred in July 1992 in the area of Basildon in Essex. Even more bizarrely, this event unfolded on a clear summer's day.

During the afternoon of 28 July 1992, large piles of straw were reported to be raining down from the sky. This phenomenon was believed to be connected to a similar 'straw fall' on the same day in South Wonston in Hampshire. Though there are many theories as to what causes these strange showers, a satisfactory explanation for this particular case has yet to be given.

Crisis Apparitions

The term 'crisis apparition' refers to the manifestation of a person who, at the time of their appearance, is undergoing some form of crisis. This may be a severe illness, an injury or even death. The vision of the manifestation is usually seen by somebody close to them.

The theory behind this phenomenon is that the afflicted person (the sender or agent), who is either ill or dying, telepathically sends out an image of themselves to someone who has a close relationship with them. It is thought that in general the sender or agent is unconscious or unaware of sending any message. However, in the case of a death crisis where the sender/agent actually dies, this is clearly difficult to verify. The most common crisis apparition is usually the death apparition which has led people to also coin the term 'living ghost' in reference to these phenomena.

A fascinating example of a crisis apparition occurred at Langley Manor in Great Waltham in 1623. One day, quite inexplicably, the daughter of Sir Charles Lee announced that she had seen her dead mother in the building, who had told her she would die the following day. Understandably unnerved by this, the family called in doctors to examine the girl who, after examination, was given a clean bill of health. The following day Sir Charles's daughter was found dead. Her cause of death was pronounced as 'unknown'.

An unequally unnerving and more macabre crisis manifestation appeared to a mother at Great Codham Hall in Wethersfield in the early 1700s. Early on a February morning the woman awoke to be greeted by the blood soaked spirit of her son standing over her bed. She ran screaming from her room and spent the next few hours being comforted by other members of the household. It was only later that day that she received the news that her son had been killed in a duel the previous night.

Some crisis apparitions are not known to the person they visit. A witness can even stumble upon an apparition meant for somebody else. Sometimes this can have disastrous consequences, as is the case with the following account.

Burghstead Lodge is currently a Registry Office and Library Archive in Billericay. The eighteenth-century Georgian house has a vast history, part of which involves a particularly disturbing haunting involving a crisis apparition. During the 1800s a nurse was given the job of attending to a sick man in the lodge, who wasn't given much hope of making a recovery. On two consecutive evenings the nurse saw a veiled woman in a green gown standing over the man's sick bed. As the nurse entered the room and approached the woman she vanished. The nurse had no idea who or what the woman was, but what she did know was that the woman was not a member of, or visitor to, the manor at the time. On the third evening, during a visit to the room to attend to her patient, the nurse once again saw the woman in the green gown. This time the nurse hurried over to the woman and removed her veil. What the nurse saw beneath the woman's veil is not known, but the patient was found dead the following morning and the nurse was in such a state of distress following her encounter that she was eventually pronounced insane. Within months of witnessing the crisis apparition the nurse had died too.

The Mysterious Fire

On Saturday, 27 August 1938, Chelmsford City Football Club's supporters' group were holding a dance at Shire Hall in Chelmsford. Twenty-two-year-old Phyllis Newcombe and her fiancé Henry McAusland were amongst those attending the party that night. The dance ended at around midnight and a few minutes after the crowds began leaving the hall Phyllis and Henry made their way out too. Henry was a few steps in front of Phyllis and, as he reached the staircase, he heard a terrifying scream from behind him. He turned around and saw the bottom front of Phyllis's dress was on fire.

Phyllis ran back to the ballroom, where some people were still milling around and still ablaze, stumbled back into the ballroom and collapsed in the entrance. Some of the revellers ran to aid Phyllis, smothering her in coats to try and extinguish the fire. An ambulance was called, which arrived within twenty minutes and Phyllis was taken to Chelmsford Hospital. She was diagnosed with serious burns on her legs, arms and chest.

At first she seemed to be making a recovery, but her wounds became septic, which led to her contracting pneumonia. Eventually she died. The tragic death of this poor girl was to cause quite a stir among the sceptics and the believers within the paranormal community. Was this a case of spontaneous human combustion (the name used to describe alleged cases of the burning of a living human body without an apparent external source of ignition)? Or was this an unfortunate, explainable accident?

Immediately after the incident there was conjecture that the dress had caught fire through contact with a cigarette end or a lighted match thrown down from a higher place above the stairs. Witnesses claimed they hadn't seen anybody there and besides, a match thrown from the balcony over the staircase would surely have been extinguished before it reached the floor. Also relevant was the fact that Phyllis' dress caught fire on a spot not directly underneath that balcony. L.F. Beccle, the coroner of the case, theorised that the fire was probably caused by a burning match on the ground. In a retrospective look into the case for a 2001 edition of *The Skeptical Inquirer* Jan Willem Nienhuys wrote that:

> Smoking was not allowed in the ballroom, but the normal behaviour of smokers is to light up as soon as they leave a non-smoking area (they don't drop many cigarette ends then). They light their cigarettes with a match and extinguish the match, for example with a habitual wrist movement and then drop it unthinkingly. The match will go out immediately when it hits a stone floor.
>
> However, when the match falls on a somewhat softer surface it occasionally stays burning for up to five seconds. The floor at the exit of the ballroom was described by the coroner as made of rubber and a witness testified that a lighted match on the floor could go on burning. If my conjecture is correct, the source of the fire was a match thrown on the floor by someone who walked at most five steps in front of her. Phyllis was an indirect victim of nicotinism.

Keeping in mind the distinct possibility that a discarded match was the cause of the fire, Coroner Beccle asked whether a burnt match was found at the location. Police Constable

Shire Hall, Chelmsford, where an alleged case of spontaneous human combustion took place in 1938.

Thorogood, who had been at the scene, stated that he hadn't found any burnt matches or cigarette butts in the area where Phyllis' dress caught fire. Following the accident Phyllis' father George had been experimenting with a piece of material that was almost identical to that of the dress that Phyllis had worn on the night of her death. He found that it wouldn't catch fire by contact with a burning cigarette, let alone by a falling cigarette end or by the hem of the dress sweeping over it. George Newcombe repeated this test in front of Coroner L.F. Beccle. Even though Henry McAusland (Phyllis' boyfriend) added that perhaps the dress might have acquired extra combustibility from the vapours of a chemical cleaning agent used six weeks earlier, Beccle dismissed this theory commenting, 'In all my experience I have not met anything so very mysterious as this.'

The story of Phyllis Newcombe has been told in various books and magazines all over the world. The facts vary and have become to some extent embellished, depending on what version you read. Sceptics believe that there is a logical answer as to how Phyllis's dress caught fire that night and others would attribute the course of the fire to a rather more paranormal source.

The fact is this terrible tragedy really did happen, whether it was a case of a discarded match, a cigarette butt or of spontaneous human combustion, we may never know for sure.

The Georgian House

In 1946, a brother and sister were walking a familiar path in woodland between Leigh-on-Sea and Hadleigh. During their walk they spotted a building that was unfamiliar to them. They approached the building and saw that it was a Georgian house that they had never seen before. A girl dressed in 'old fashioned' clothes walked down the driveway accompanied by her dog and passed them. As she passed the girl seemed oblivious to the brother and sister.

Upon returning home the siblings were unable to locate the house on any maps and later they were unable to find the house at all. A study conducted by the Society for Psychical Research on this case suggests that the witnesses were mistaken and the house in fact does exist, yet the brother and sister were convinced they had in fact endured a time slip (travelling through time via some unknown paranormal phenomena) and had experienced a scene from a bygone era.

Backward Gravity

On a stretch of road in Epping, it is in fact possible to travel by car to the bottom of a hill, release your handbrake and roll back up to the top. There are two theories as to why this happens. The first is that this location is in fact a gravity hill, also known as a magnetic hill (and sometimes a mystery hill or a gravity road). These hills are places where the layout of the surrounding land produces the optical illusion that a very slight downhill slope appears to be an uphill slope. Thus, a car left out of gear will appear to be rolling uphill. Another theory, held by those that have encountered other ghostly goings on in the area, such as sightings of apparitions, believe the fact that a lot of cars come to a stop at the site of the old gallows after rolling up the hill suggests that this phenomena is indeed paranormal.

Crop Circles

A crop circle is a sizable pattern created by the flattening of a crop such as wheat, barley, rye, maize, or rapeseed. Since appearing in the media in the 1970s, crop circles have become the subject of speculation by various paranormal, ufological, and anomalistic investigators, ranging from proposals that they were created by bizarre meteorological phenomena to suggestions that they were messages from extraterrestrials.

The location of many crop circles near ancient sites such as Stonehenge and chalk horses, has led many New Age belief systems to incorporate crop circles, often relating them to ley lines. Some New Age supporters have arbitrarily related crop circles to the Gaia hypothesis, alleging that Gaia, the earth, is actually alive and that crop circles are messages or responses to stimuli such as global warming and human pollution. It asserts that the earth may be modelled as if a single super-organism, in that earthly components (e.g. biota, climate, temperature, sunlight, etc.) influence each other and are organised to function and develop as a whole.

The main criticism of the alleged non-human creation of crop circles is that while evidence is essentially absent (besides eyewitness testimonies), some are definitely known to be the work of human pranksters and others could be adequately explained as such. There have been cases in which researchers have declared crop circles to be 'the real thing', only to be confronted with the people who created the circle and documented the fraud. Most notably in 1991, Doug Bower and Dave Chorley stated that they had started the phenomenon in 1978 by making actual circles on crops with the use of simple tools. They went on to demonstrate how this hoax could be done. Many others since have also demonstrated how complex crop circles can be created. The late American astronomer and astrophysicist Carl Sagan discussed alien-based theories of crop circle formation. Sagan concluded that no empirical evidence existed to link UFOs with crop circles. Specifically, he pointed out that there were no credible cases of UFOs being observed creating a circle, yet there were many cases when it was known that human agents, such as Doug Bower and Dave Chorley, were responsible.

Having established what crop circles are and the seemingly irrefutable evidence that they are man-made, there are those that remain unexplained. There is also the fact that there are several cases of crop circles that pre-date the hoaxers of the 1970s, including a case from Essex.

In 1931 a boy and a farmer in Essex witnessed a crop circle form in a matter of seconds. The farmer attributed it to the 'Devil's twist', a kind of whirlwind blamed for similar phenomena in the area since at least 1830. Similar patterns were being reported in Essex more than 170 years later, such as the circle that appeared at Hadleigh Castle in July 2005.

Circles are not the only patterns to mysteriously appear in fields. In August 2008, Clare Bird was shocked to discover a star-shaped pattern while riding her horse near the Cherry Tree pub, in Stambridge. The pattern measured 396ft across. In an interview with the *Basildon Echo*

A sketch of the crop circle pattern which appeared in Stanbridge in 2010. (Illustration by Jason Day)

she said, 'I thought it was wheat damage at first, because I could see all this flattened corn, but the closer I got, the more I could see. It's pretty amazing. It's a star-shape, with points coming out of a centre circle.'

Strangely, another crop circle appeared in the same field five years later in August 2010. This series of patterns included several circles and geometric lines.

Man made or extra-terrestrial, the phenomenon of the crop circle continues in Essex and all across the world. Whether we will ever know for sure who or what is creating them remains to be seen.

The Soldier in the Hayloft

On Sunday, 19 February 1888, an old soldier climbed up into a hayloft in Colchester. The man had been drinking heavily and eventually had found a place to sleep off the alcohol. He was later found completely consumed by fire, while the highly flammable dry hay around him, both loose and in bundles, was not even scorched.

Doppelgangers

The term 'doppelganger' refers to the projection of oneself, a splitting of one's 'etheric twin' from your physical body, if you will. During a doppelganger manifestation the person responsible is not consciously in control of achieving this state.

The literal translation of doppelganger from its German origin is 'double walker'. Stories of doppelgangers have astounded and terrified people for thousands of years and accounts can be found in the deepest annals of history. Ancient Egyptians believed that on occasion a person's etheric double could leave their sleeping body and roam free. It is also recorded in Norse mythology that there were cases of a ghostly double, known as a vardogr, who preceded a living person and was seen performing their actions long before they actually carried them out themselves. It is said that the doppelganger has no reflection and casts no shadow, thus theoretically eliminating the possibility of a sighting being a mistaken reflection of oneself. The doppelganger is said to provide advice to the person they shadow, whether that be good guidance or misleading and harmful advice. Given that a doppelganger is generally thought of as an evil twin, it is usually the latter and it is therefore regarded as unwise to try to communicate with a doppelganger. Most alarming of all in doppelganger folklore is that apparently a doppelganger seen by a person's friends or relatives is a portent of illness or danger and to see one's own doppelganger is an omen of death.

One of the most famous cases of a doppelganger sighting in Essex took place at Colchester Hospital. An elderly, bedridden, female patient was receiving treatment in the hospital and was staying on ward eight. Her doppelganger was seen on a number of occasions around the hospital during her stay, although as was mentioned earlier, the lady was unable to leave her bed.

During the 1960s another doppelganger case was reported in the county. The figure of Mrs Punter was seen around her home in 1967 and 1969, even though she was in an entirely different room at the times of the sightings. Manifestations of the living such as these continue to baffle and intrigue paranormal investigators the world over.

Bibliography

Books

Brown, Gerry, *The World's Greatest Mysteries* (Octopus Publishing, 1986)

Fielding, Yvette & O'Keeffe, Ciaran, *Ghost Hunters: A Guide to Investigating the Paranormal* (Hodder & Stoughton, 2006)

Fraser, Mark (ed.), *Big Cats in Britain Yearbook 2008* (CFZ Press, 2008)

Matthews, Marcus, *Big Cats Loose in Britain* (CFZ Press, 2007)

McEwan, Graham J., *Mystery Animals of Britain and Ireland* (Robert Hale Ltd, 1986)

Newton, Michael, *Encyclopaedia of Cryptozoology: A Global Guide* (McFarland & Co., 2004)

Puttick, Betty, *Ghosts of Essex* (Countryside Books, 1998)

Robson, Alan, *Nightmare On Your Street: More Grisly Trails and Ghostly Tales* (Virgin Books, 1993)

Smyth, Frank & Stemman, Roy, *Mysteries of the Afterlife* (Aldus Books, 1975)

Other Sources

Colchester Daily Gazette (28 January 2009)

The *Sun* (28 October 2004)

London Illustrated News (2 December 1954)

RAF Flying Review (July 1957)

The *Sun*, 'By gum! Flattened cyclist vanishes' by Kieron Saunders (15 July 1988)

Skeptical Inquirer, Vol. 25, Issue 2, p.28-34, 'Spontaneous Human Confabulation: Requiem for Phyllis' by Jan Willem Nienhuys' (March/April 2001)

The Essex Chronicle, 'Girl in Flames at Shire Hall Dance' (2 September 1938)

The Essex Weekly News, 'A Human Torch: Chelmsford Woman Badly Burned' (2 September 1938)

The Essex Weekly News, 'Supporters' Club Dance' (2 September 1938)

Flying Saucer Review, 'The Langenhoe Incident' by Dr Bernard E. Finch (Nov-Dec 1965)

Flying Saucer Review, Vol. 23, Issue 2, 'Catalogue of Humanoid Reports, case 1977-25, (August 1977)

Alternate Perceptions, online magazine, Issue. 103, 'The Aveley Abduction, Part 1' *by* Brent Raynes *(July 2006)*

Epping Guardian, 'Could Beast of Ongar Have Left It's Mark?' (6 June 2007)

The British Medical Journal, p.841-42 (April 21 1888)
ASH magazine, Issue 4, 'Legends of Canewdon' by Mike Howard (1989)
Strange But True, television series (1993-1997)

Online Resources

Author's website (www.jasonday.co.uk)
Peter Underwood (www.peterunderwood.org.uk)
The Society for Psychical Research (www.spr.ac.uk/main)
Phantom Encounters, Paranormal Events Company (www.phantomencounters.co.uk)
Richard Felix (www.richardfelix.co.uk)
The Paranormal Database (www.paranormaldatabase.com)
Mysterious Britain (www.mysteriousbritain.co.uk)
Queen Alexandra's Royal Army Nursing Corps (www.qaranc.co.uk)
Road Ghosts (www.roadghosts.com)
The British UFO Research Association (www.bufora.org.uk)
The Centre for Fortean Zoology (www.cfz.org.uk)
The White Noise Paranormal Radio Show (www.whitenoiseparanormalradio.co.uk)
It's Only a Movie…Isn't It? (www.itsonlyamovie.webs.com)
Kelvedon Hatch Secret Nuclear Bunker (www.secretnuclearbunker.com)
Layer Marney Tower (www.layermarneytower.co.uk)
Moot Hall (www.maldonmoothall.org.uk)
The Coalhouse Fort Project (www.coalhousefort.co.uk)
The Harwich Society (www.harwich-society.co.uk)
The Arthur Findlay College (www.arthurfindlaycollege.org)
Waltham Abbey Church (www.walthamabbeychurch.co.uk)

Other titles published by The History Press

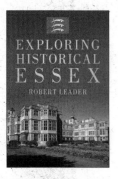

Exploring Historical Essex
ROBERT C. SMITH

Serving as both an inspiring guide and a lasting souvenir, this book paints a comprehensive picture of Essex, with fascinating historical tales and secrets from its past. Exploring the county's marvellous maritime heritage, the book follows all of the major rivers from their sources to the sea. From the Colne Valley to golden Saffron Walden, it describes historic castles, great abbeys, stately homes, windmills, churches, by-ways and oysters, enriched with striking images that bring historical Essex to life.

978 0 7524 5764 2

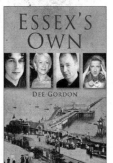

Essex's Own
DEE GORDON

Athlete Sally Gunnell, painter Edward Bawden, actress Joan Sims, singer Billy Bragg, footballer Bobby Moore, chef Jamie Oliver, playwright Sarah Kane, and the infamous highwayman Dick Turpin are among personalities who have been born in Essex through the ages. This book features mini-biographies of all these and many more, including those who lived here and left their mark on the area, such as authors Douglas Adams and comedian Lee Evans. Prepare for a fascinating read for residents and visitors alike.

978 0 7509 5121 0

Haunted Essex
CARMEL KING

From heart-stopping accounts of apparitions, manifestations and related supernatural phenomena, to first-hand encounters with phantoms and spirits, *Haunted Essex* contains a chilling range of ghostly phenomena. Featuring the well-known story of Robin the Woodcutter of Coggeshall and the tale of how Thundersley's 'Shrieking Boy's Wood' acquired its name, this phenomenal gathering of ghostly goings-on, drawn from both historical and contemporary sources, is bound to captivate.

978 0 7524 5126 8

Haunted Scunthorpe
JASON DAY

Including previously unpublished accounts from Jason Day's own case files, this gripping book guides you through Scunthorpe's paranormal hotspots and follows the apparitions into the surrounding villages and beyond. Including the most documented poltergeist case in history, this collection of local hauntings recounts cases both past and present from the author's home-town. Whether it be a public house, a deserted road, a desolate graveyard or a family home, it would seem that *Haunted Scunthorpe* has a ghost for every location.

978 0 7524 5521 1

Visit our website and discover thousands of other History Press books.
www.thehistorypress.co.uk